United States Judo Association

Coach Education Program - Level 1

Dr. Christopher Dewey

Coach Education Program– Level 1
Copyright © 2005 By Christopher Dewey

All rights reserved.

Printed in the United States of America. No part of this book may be used or reproduced in any manner whatsoever without written permission except in the case of brief quotations embodied in critical articles and reviews.

For information, address Fifth Estate, Post Office Box 116, Blountsville, AL 35031.

Designed by Matt Owens

Printed on acid-free paper

Library of Congress Control No: 2005921125

ISBN: 0-9760992-4-1

Fifth Estate
2005

ABOUT THE AUTHOR

Dr. Chris Dewey is a 35-year veteran of the martial arts and holds the rank of sixth degree black belt in both Judo and Ju Jitsu, as well the rank of third degree black belt in Hapkido and fourth degree black belt in Taekwondo. Chris is an active coach, referee and competitor and was the USJA Coach of the Year in 1998. Chris has been competing for more than thirty years and has won national championships in both kata (forms) and master's shiai (free fighting). Chris has been teaching martial arts for more than twenty years in community, grade school and university settings and is the owner and chief instructor of the Starkville Martial Arts Academy. Chris is the Mississippi faculty member for the National Association of Professional Martial Artists, National School Support Network and is a regular columnist in the MAPro magazine.

Although born and educated in England, Chris obtained his doctorate in Geology in Canada. He moved to Mississippi in 1984 and has held a faculty position in Geosciences at Mississippi State University ever since. Chris also holds an adjunct position in the Department of Kinesiology.

In other activities, Chris is also a certified Toastmaster, a certified Reiki Master, an avid reader and a published poet. During his spare time Chris treasures his wife, Janet, and son, Graham.

United States Judo Association Coaching Education Program

Acknowledgements

Judo has changed my life for the better in so many ways that I honestly have no idea how to write this section. Given that I have been active in the martial arts since 1968 and hold black belt rank in four different styles, it would be virtually impossible for me to give due thanks to all the people to whom I owe a debt of gratitude. I have been blessed to receive instruction from some outstanding instructors over the years and from their examples I have learned much. Equally, teaching goes both ways and I have learned so much from my own students that I could not possibly begin to thank them all one by one.

I would not be here, writing this were it not for my parents who put me on the martial road all those years ago, with a simple enough question: "Do you want to learn Judo?" But perhaps I should also thank all those bullies who led my parents to ask the question in the first place.

Roy Inman is one of the great British Olympic coaches and was my first sensei. He actually came to our house to visit with my parents and I before I joined his club and took my first Judo lesson. How many coaches can say that they have visited with their potential students before they had even signed up? Roy, I have never thanked you for opening the door and guiding those first steps. I do not know how I could possibly thank you enough.

I want to thank George Weers who has mentored me in coaching within the USJA and also the members of the Coaching Education Committee, who keep me on the straight and narrow. Particularly, I would like to thank my Vice Chair, Gerry Lafon, for asking me the questions that make me squirm and for giving me a dose of reality every once in a while. To the coaches and instructors around the country who have given me feedback, I can only tell you that my thanks are reflected in the positive changes that your comments have elicited in the manuals and without your feedback, these manuals would be lacking. I have valued your candor and your honesty; and because of your questions, insights and concerns, everyone benefits. I would be remiss in not thanking the leadership of the USJA both past and present, who gave me the opportunity of leading the Coaching Education Committee and the task of carrying forward the coaching program from those who held that responsibility before me.

Lastly, my wife Janet and my son Graham have brought a color and texture to my world that I could not have imagined. Janet has shared her insights with me and supported me through my times of doubt and shared in my times of triumph. Her wisdom and love have been a constant marvel to me.

We all stand on the shoulders of giants to see our world. To each of you, named here or not, I cannot possibly give to you the honor or repay the debt that I owe you. If these manuals help to improve Judo in some small way, or give the opportunity of a new life to a struggling child, then I will have said thank you to each of you in the only way I know that will make a lasting change.

Thank you.

Preface

The United States Judo Association Coach Education Program exists to help **you**, the coach. The series of courses within the program will not teach you how to do a technique, so much as prepare you to impart your knowledge more effectively. Regardless of your coaching aim, your primary goal is to recruit and retain students. Our goal is to provide you with the tools necessary to help you build American Judo and to help you be a force for positive change in the lives of your students. As a coach, sensei, instructor, teacher or whatever you call yourself, you touch the lives of the students that come to you for training. We want to help you perform that task in the most positive, effective and efficient fashion possible. If you want to be a successful Judo coach you will need more than excellent technique and a desire to teach, although these are both indispensable. Being a successful Judo coach is as much about your personal desire for continuing your own education as it is about what you have to offer your students. Just because you have excellent technical skill or a room full of competition honors, does not necessarily mean that you can convey your knowledge to a willing student in an effective manner. Consequently, if you wish to become a truly successful Judo coach, it is important that you acquire the skills required of a successful teacher. This is where the USJA Coach Education Program can help you. We are here to help you in the process of becoming a better coach. It is your journey and your path, we are merely providing some tools to help you along the way.

From a pedagogic perspective, coaching Judo is no different to teaching any other curriculum. Learning Judo requires that every student acquires a set of skills for advancement to different levels and involves him or herself in a process of continual investigation, which leads to higher levels of mastery. Unlike other areas of teaching, which may be predominantly physical or entirely mental, the teacher of Judo has the potential to profoundly affect the student's cognitive awareness, psychomotor abilities, emotional awareness and social skills.

Please remember this: The USJA Coach Education Program is **your** program. We solicit your input and your feedback. We value your opinion. Because you are the coaches on the front line building American Judo we want to know how we can help you do the job. Our success will be measured by the growth of American Judo.

Thank you for choosing our program and welcome.

"We are what we repeatedly do. Excellence then, is not an act, but a habit."

Aristotle

Table of Contents

- Acknowledgements — ii
- Preface — vi
- Table of Contents — x
- List of Appendices — xii
- Welcome — xiv
- So What? I Don't Teach Judo — xvi
- Rationale for the USJA Coach Education Program — xviii

Level I Content:

- Conditions of Learning — 2
- Psychology of Learning — 26
- Safety in the Dojo — 38
- Legal Considerations — 54
- Physical Principles — 76
- Tournaments — 112
- Conclusion — 120

References — 122

Appendices — 126

List of Appendices

- Information about the USJA Coaching Education Program   128
- Waiver   140
- Risk Agreement   142
- Health History   148
- Sample Blood Policy   150
- Sample Double Elimination Pool Sheet   152
- Sample Round Robin Pool Sheet   153

Welcome

Thank you for choosing the United States Judo Association Coach Education Program. This is a team effort. We are not here to tell you how to do Seoi Nage, or even give you drills to teach. We are here to provide information about how to teach and how to create a learning environment that keeps your students coming back for more. You have already invested a good deal of time in acquiring the skills of a quality Judoka. You have earned the respect of your peers and now you find yourself in the position of an instructor. For some of you, instruction may be a new experience. Some of you may have been coaching Judo for decades. To all of you we say this: The biggest room in the world is the room for improvement and that applies to all of us. The Coach Education Committee applauds your decision to take this course and if we can help you in any way, please feel free to contact us through the national office or through the USJA Web Site at http://www.usja-judo.org. Whether you are a novice coach or a veteran campaigner, we hope that this course contains something new for you. Even if "you've heard it all before", maybe there is a new slant for you or a new way of looking at things that can spur you onward to higher levels of performance.

So What? I Don't Teach Judo

Whether you teach Judo or not, the USJA Coaching Education Program offers you valuable information about teaching martial arts, regardless of style. Currently, coaches, club owners and instructors in **Aikido, Hapkido, Isshinryu, Ju Jitsu, Shotokan, Taekwondo, and T'ai Chi** have completed the USJA Coaching courses. We have also had martial arts and **defense tactics instructors** in various branches of the armed forces and law enforcement establishments complete our courses. Although we may not be teaching you how to teach a better sidekick or arresting technique, these courses will offer you insights into how you may be able to improve the quality of the training experiences your players and students receive. It does not matter whether you teach a for profit or non-profit business, a recreational martial arts school, the bottom line always comes back to your ability to **attract** and **retain** students. Some of our coaches deal with audiences who are required to take their courses, but this does not alter the need to offer a learning experience that is both **meaningful** and **appropriate** for the needs of the student. One of the great arbiters of your success is what your current students say about what you offer in your program and how it is delivered. The USJA Coaching Education Program exists to help you improve the quality of what you offer to your students, so that you will be able to keep them for longer and take them further down the road of learning.

Rationale for the USJA Coach Education Program

In 1974, Ben Campbell published a little book called Championship Judo Drill Training. On page 14 of this book we find a call to action:

> *"It is about time, however, that American Judoists put some common sense and realism into their training methods. I say it is about time because our relative standing in world Judo is very low and falling lower (about 20th in 1971, 1972, and 1973 – Editor)"*

It would be wonderful to report that since Ben wrote his book, things have changed, but this is not the case, especially in light of the fact that U.S. Judo finished 41st at the 2001 World Games in Munich. Furthermore, in a very revealing of the history of Black Belt magazine, Graden and Callos (2001), drew attention to three facts concerning Judo, namely: i) that volume 1, number 1 of Black Belt magazine, in 1961 featured a cover story on the AAU National Judo Championships, ii) that by the end of 1966 a survey showed that "karate players" had surpassed "judo players" by a figure of 113,000 to 75,000, and lastly iii) that in the eighties, judo which had been a mainstay of the magazine since its inception was almost phased out. The call to action therefore still stands, and this is all the rationale we need for the development of a coach education program.

More than ever, the need exists to evaluate what we are doing as Judo coaches and how we are doing it, because clearly, we are not recruiting large numbers of the population to Judo, nor are we retaining those we recruit and neither are we producing large numbers of world champions. There is a maxim in business, which says if you like the results you are getting continue doing what you are doing.

If we look at the membership statistics, according to the three main Judo organizations in the United States, namely the United States Judo Association, United States Judo Incorporated (National Governing Body) and the United States Judo Federation, there are fewer than 30,000 people currently training in Judo. The fact that 30,000 people "do" Judo in a country with a population of more than 270,000,000 is a sad testament to our ability to recruit and retain students. According to industry statistics, only about 1% of the American population studies a martial art of any kind. If thirty thousand people study Judo then that represents about 0.0012% of the American population.

What is truly sad about this statistic is that many countries can boast half a million or more Judoka despite having much smaller populations from which to draw.

Each of us who has put twenty or thirty years or more into Judo knows that it has changed our lives for the better. Yet despite the many benefits that we see in our own lives in terms of mental and physical fitness, Judo as a sport or a martial art does not seem to be retaining those it recruits. The responsibility for this situation must fall squarely on the shoulders of all of us who teach and coach. It does not matter whether we are teaching for recreation or tournament, sport or art. If we are not keeping the students we recruit, then there must be room for improvement in what we do and how we do it.

The USJA Coach Education Committee recognizes that part of the challenge is that while students are learning Judo, they are not learning how to pass on what they learn. Consequently, when many students assume the mantle of leadership in the form of a coaching responsibility for the first time, they often find themselves woefully unprepared. As a natural solution for the problem, we fall back on the tried and true…it worked for me; it'll work for you. Unfortunately that is rarely true and frequently causes us to lose many of the students we would love to keep. The rationale for developing the USJA Coach Education Program was to deliberately seek mechanisms through which coaches could gain access to information that would better prepare them for passing on the knowledge that they had acquired. The program has existed since the late 1970's. Its early pioneers were Eli Morrell and Wally Marr. From 1986 until 2001, the last chairman, George Weers, worked tirelessly to provide manuals that explained the conditions necessary to create a functional and positive learning environment as well as expose the principles that govern the sport of Judo as well as providing a framework for the long-term development of players.

As we move forward, this program will endeavor to provide you with relevant coaching information regardless of whether you are coaching children or adults, men or women, competitors or recreational players. There is a place in Judo for all of us, and there are ways in which we can make that place home and derive a lifetime's benefit from being in Judo.

The Level I Coaching Course

I. Conditions of Learning

When we teach, we create an environment in which the student must learn. It follows, therefore that regardless of the subject material, there are particular attributes of the learning environment, which when present, will facilitate the learning process. As a coach, you are responsible and accountable for both the creation of an effective learning environment and the content of the lessons. The level to which you ensure that each of the conditions of learning is met during each class and for each lesson plan, controls the degree to which you will be successful in getting your message across to your students. There are twelve conditions necessary for the creation of a positive learning environment (Gagne, Briggs and Wager, 1992; Martens, 1990; Weers, 1995, Wilen et al, 2000). Of these, establishing goals must rank as the most important. In its simplest form, if you do not know what you want your students to learn it is impossible to proceed with the learning process.

Goal Setting: Goal setting is an integral part of all measured progress. To a greater or lesser extent we all like to have some idea of where we are going and what we are doing. The same is true of your students. Without achieving set goals, your students will become uncertain of where they are going and will lose motivation.

Looked at from the educational perspective, goal setting can be divided into four distinct aspects:

i). <u>Student expectations</u>: First, what are the students' spoken or unspoken expectations of being in the Judo class? Ask yourself as a coach, why are these players in my class? Do I know? Am I providing what they are seeking? Are they seeking what I am willing and/or able to teach? Meeting the students' goals provides meaningful reasons for continuing the process of training, it is therefore important to know why your students are in class in the first place. If the instructor is unaware of the student's goals in training it will be difficult at best to develop a true working relationship.

ii). <u>In-class performance goals</u>: The second aspect of goal setting is the practical performance goal associated with any given exercise or technique in a lesson plan. These types of goals are necessarily very specific, short-term goals that lead to satisfaction in class. On a class by class basis, performance goals allow both student and instructor to measure the degree to which a training drill has been successfully executed. Any performance goal must be **specific, challenging but attainable, performance oriented** and **measurable**. One of the major keys here is that the goal should be challenging enough to motivate your students and measurable so that the students can see exactly how close they are to achieving the goal. Moreover, a performance goal must be very specific, allowing no room for ambiguity by the student, the coach, or in the ability to measure the goal. Performance goals must be based upon what the students do, and not dependent upon an outcome beyond their immediate control. A measurable performance goal for a biomechanical action might include the correct foot or body position. By way of contrast in a tournament situation, an appropriate goal might be to make a specified number of attacks with a skill during a given time interval. Obtaining a specific score during a tournament is dependent upon outside factors over which the player has no control, is therefore outcome related and consequently not a reasonable goal. Whether being used in the dojo during class or on the mat during competition, performance goals must be things that lie within the student's immediate sphere of control. To summarize and drive home the point: **The student can control where he or she places his or her body during the application of a skill and the number of times a skill is attempted during a tournament match. The student cannot control what score, if any, a referee might award for a successful technique**.

Figure 1: Goal Setting. Obtaining a specific score during a tournament is dependent upon outside factors, is therefore outcome related and consequently not a reasonable goal.

iii). <u>Long-term goals</u>: A third set of goals relates to how your lesson plans fit into a long-term program of study that will lead to higher levels of mastery. Every lesson plan should be a step in the process of getting to a specific goal and presupposes the existence of some sort of long-range plan such as achieving a certain level of rank or competitive ability. As an example, let us use achieving a Black belt as our long-term plan. Each requirement for any given rank is an action step within the single goal of obtaining the next rank and should be reflected in your lesson plan sequence. Obviously, each rank is a stair step of progress and a measurable indicator of how close a student is to his or her goal. When a White Belt steps on to the mat for the first time, setting a goal of Black Belt may be very commendable, but it is a nebulous goal based on a lack of information. A much more specific and attainable goal as a novice player is to achieve Yellow Belt and that goal can be broken down into learning the requirements necessary for advancement with an expectation of completing those steps within a specified time window, given regular attendance at class. Once the student has achieved the first goal, it becomes easier to establish loftier goals with the assurance of achieving the desired result given dedication, perseverance and hard work. If an analogy would be useful, then each lesson plan is a section of road and the long-term plan is the road map you will use to guide your students from novice players to their chosen destination. If you have no idea what you will be teaching next week, how is the student going to know how useful this week's lesson plan will be to their overall growth and development? Long-term planning will be introduced in the Level II Course and explored in detail in Level III.

iv). <u>Coaching goals</u>: The last set of goals that affect the conditions of learning are the goals that you have as a coach. Ask yourself why you are teaching Judo. What do you want to achieve? Sometimes, these goals may be competing with each other: For instance if you want to teach recreational Judo and also produce a national champion, we would suggest to you that you have competing teaching goals. It follows therefore, that you must have clear coaching goals, and furthermore, those goals will inevitably affect the types of students that you recruit. If you want to run a recreational club, that's fine, but don't then take your players to tournament and berate them for a lack luster performance against players from a club which lives and breathes tournament participation. Clearly, your teaching goals must be congruent with your philosophical goals.

Movement: It is impossible to learn Judo by standing still (Campbell, 1974; Weers, 1995). When Judo takes place in a real life self-defense scenario or in the highly charged tournament arena, it occurs in very fluid and volatile environments. Students need to be aware of the importance of movement from the first moment they step on the mat.

At beginning levels of performance introduce large body actions and gross motor principles such as keeping the hands in front of the hips, combined with an ability to produce an effective push. As students become more aware of their movement abilities start to refine position and deal with the minor stuff. If you demonstrate correct movement and your students imitate the large actions correctly, the minor aspects will often be self-correcting. Above all, give your students time to experiment with movement and to find the answers themselves before you rush in to correct minor details.

Judo primarily deals with understanding how to control balance and force. Consequently, learning Judo becomes a problem of cause and effect. Every time a student moves an effect is created. Eventually, the successful students will learn to control the effects, which they create as a result of their actions. There is nothing arbitrary when two people are working together in a Judo class. If one person initiates an action, a response is created in his or her partner and so on. The goal therefore, is to bring each student to an awareness of the cause and effect relationship of his or her actions. This understanding lies at the very heart of good randori and shiai performance.

Activity: A good instructional rule to follow is 85% student activity, 15% instructor explanation. Students come to you to learn and to train, they do not come to hear your war stories or watch you perform. Your students need and want direct experience, so make sure that you let them have as much training time as possible. Personal experience in Judo is the best possible way to learn, which means that students will obtain the maximum benefit from "doing" not "watching". Active and vibrant classes also serve to maintain student interest, create positive endorphin responses and enhance retention. Make your instructional segments succinct, demonstrate what you need to with precision and brevity, ask for questions and then let the students practice.

The best thing that you can do for your students is to let them experiment and learn for themselves. Once you have given a task, together with its performance goal let your students have as much practice time as possible, let them figure things out for themselves and offer guidance when needed. As a safety tip, there is a decreased likelihood of injury if students are warm and stay warm through continued activity.

Simplicity: Success becomes possible for your students when you give precise direction in the execution of simple drills at the outset and allow plenty of time for practice. Create a clear expectation in the minds of your students and they will know what is expected and what to achieve. Recurring success in simple drills leads to improvements in student competence combined with a desire for more complex tasks. Competence leads to confidence, and it is this improvement in self-confidence that will enable the student to tackle more complex tasks. Giving complex tasks before the student is adequately prepared will create confusion and frustration, which will also lead to the erosion of confidence and trust placed in the instructor by the student. The erosion of trust will lead inevitably to a high drop out rate.

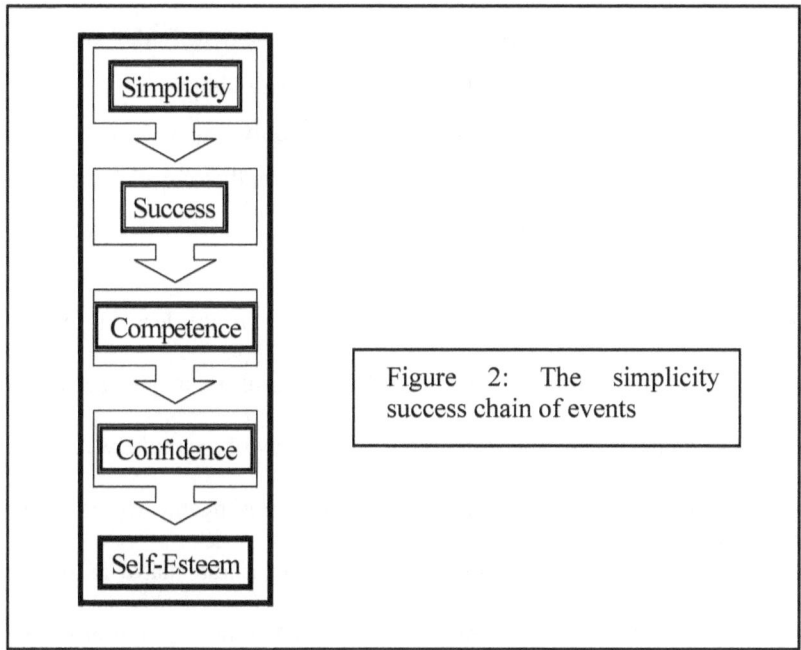

Figure 2: The simplicity success chain of events

In summary, keep demonstrations simple, emphasize the key elements several times and ensure understanding by the student. There are several things that an instructor can do to enhance simplicity:

    i)   Recognize the need to start with simple drills.
    ii)   Decide what performance goals should be emphasized for a given class segment.
    iii)   Be sensitive to how much information the class can handle.
    iv)   Be willing to repeat your instructions, explain yourself in a different way or alter a lesson plan.
    v)   Provide plenty of time for practice.

vi) Be prepared to modify tasks according to individual needs.
vii) Provide specific, reinforcement of correct execution.
viii) Understand that what one student finds "simple" is not what all students might see as simple.
ix) Build complex drills only after creating a solid foundation with simple tasks that have been successfully completed.

Series and Sequence: Mastery of the subject matter in any learning endeavor is demonstrated by the ability to abstract information from a data set and create meaningful sequences using the available data. By way of example, we may teach a student the words of a language, but it is only by putting the words together to create a meaningful communication in an effective fashion that a mastery of the language is demonstrated. In general, we tend to recognize that the more fluid the communication, the greater the degree of mastery. We can apply this analogy to the extent that the practice of Judo is a form of communication. The greater the degree of grace and efficiency with which the elements of the language (Judo) are manipulated, the higher level of mastery.

Continuing the analogy, no informational component of a language stands on its own. Consequently, the techniques that we teach in Judo must be part of a series, not a syllabus of isolated movements that share no connectivity to one another.

At the lowest level of investigation, a series as used in a Judo drill could consist of the individual parts of a single technique such as movement, gripping exchange, entry to the throw, balance control, moment of throw and finish (e.g. to hold down). In the Kodokan Judo (Kano, 1986; Weers, 2003), all throws consist of three parts:

      i)   Kuzushi or developing an off-balance,
      ii)   Tsukuri or fitting to the throw
      iii)   Kake or the moment of throw.

There is also a fourth part to all throws: Zanshin or the finish. Literally, zanshin means the remaining spirit. Additionally, consider the possibility that the off-balance and the fitting to the throw portions are actually performed in reverse order. Before we do anything useful in Judo we move and often we create the off-balance as we fully commit to the throw. Our training partners and competition opponents are dynamic persons who will not stand still and wait for us to enter the throw, once they find themselves off-balance. For sure, when we teach, we isolate movements within the drill such as the correct off-balance and such, yet in the volatile and dynamic setting of the training environment moves are not discrete and isolated actions. Aristotle's law of cause and effect is always in operation and the successful students will be the ones who understand how to work the law to their advantage.

Be that as it may, although we can demonstrate that a throw is composed of a series of discrete actions, a technique standing alone, serves little purpose. It is only when a technique is added to others that the language of Judo comes to life. Series-based teaching requires that we do not teach our skills in isolation, but rather show how the pieces of the language fit together as a meaningful whole. For example: A series consisting of seven events might begin with initial movement to obtain a power grip which leads to a throwing opportunity being met by a counter followed by a combination into a ground hold, with an escape (Figure 3).

It is only your imagination, your willingness to research and experiment and the degree to which you encourage your students to do likewise that limit the possibilities for the creation of effective sequences.

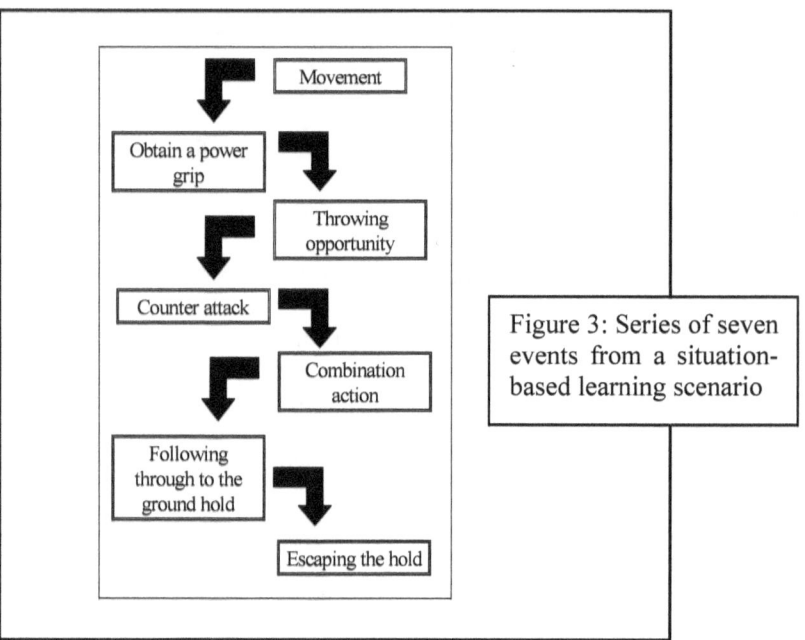

Figure 3: Series of seven events from a situation-based learning scenario

Teaching by series and sequence presupposes that there are some elements of the syllabus that need to be taught prior to other elements. This necessarily means that we begin with the simple and work up to the more complex drills. Teaching by series and sequence also ensures that we will build a solid foundation and also create meaning in our classes.

Foundation: Begin with the simple, and build a solid foundation. In so doing however, do not forget that what you, the coach might consider to be simple, will not necessarily be what your students view as simple. A lot of times, we can be quite surprised by the results generated in the real time setting of the mat. For instance, how many of us teach O Soto Gari to our white belts? Most of us, right? Now ask yourself this: How many of us actually performed O Soto Gari as a white belt? What is it that we are really doing? You can tell your beginners to "sweep" the support leg from the outside all you want, but many beginners will put the attack foot down behind their partner's leg and push their opponent over it. What most beginners perform bears more resemblance to O Soto Otoshi, than to O Soto Gari. So the point is simple: Teach the principle of what you want as the foundation and don't worry so much about taxonomic issues. The principles in this case are to attack the support foot and to push the opponent into a hole situated behind the support foot. Part of the problem in this particular instance is that many of our beginning students have not yet learned to control their own balance at that level of development, let alone be able to control their opponent's position and trajectory through space while standing on one leg.

From what we are saying here, it should be clear that solid foundations are often principle-based, rather than technique-based. As such, a principle-based foundation will provide the necessary links from the simple, beginning drills to the more complex, advanced drills. **When you develop a syllabus for your students think more about what <u>skills</u> you want them to perform rather than whether they can accomplish a specifically named throw.** If you can build a foundational base, your students will almost inevitably invent the throws for themselves. All you then have to give is a set of names, which will act as a common frame of reference in communication. For those of you who like to give names to things, give your beginning students O Soto Otoshi as a foundation skill and then add O Soto Gari as a higher-level skill when your players have acquired the necessary control. Those of you who teach children will no doubt smile when you think about how your younger beginning students in the 6-8 year old range will have difficulty remembering the name of the throw let alone performing the correct biomechanical actions.

There is another aspect of this discussion that bears mention at this point, that relates to reinforcement and retention: When we teach students "O Soto Gari" before they have the biomechanical skill or kinesthetic awareness to perform the technique, we are setting them up for failure. This is especially true if we criticize the inability to perform the "required" technique rather than praise our students for successfully mastering a foundation skill. When students do not perceive personal success, we are giving them reasons to quit.

As a word of caution, never teach anything that you will have to "unteach" later. If you ask your students to do something that you will ask them not to do later, you are building confusion and frustration. Let me give you a common example: A child goes to tournament and gets thrown for a reasonable score. The child slaps the mat and the referee awards Ippon. The match is over; the child cries and goes to his coach. The coach then scolds the child for slapping the mat and says something like "How many times have I told you not to slap the mat when you get thrown?" This is an often-repeated cycle, which will eventually drive the child and his or her parents out of Judo. Why? The answer is simple: In class the child slaps the mat every time he or she gets thrown. The child's behavior has been conditioned by repetition to a level of instinctive action. What we are dealing with here is called a "Pavlovian response" and involves a conditioned behavioral response (Ormond, 1999). To then give a contradictory command for a similar situation is to ask the child to go against everything his or her body has learned. The new command is doomed to failure from the outset. The best solution is to teach children to use the skills that will be needed (such as turnouts, which will down grade a score in a tournament setting), from the very beginning of their training.

Transference: The foregoing example leads neatly into the condition of learning known as transference. Simply put, students like to know that what they are learning has application to how it will be used in the "real world". The skills our students learn may have transference to any one of a number of areas of their lives, not the least of which includes competition and self-defense. In the physical domain, it is critical to teach those skills that have transference to the expected environment of performance. Almost as important is to practice under conditions that approximate as closely as possible the conditions under which the skill will be used, as soon as possible.

A second aspect of transference lies in the recognition that there are principles, which govern the movement of a human body in the fluid environment of a Judo class. These basic principles can be applied to **all** aspects of Judo. The basic biomechanical principles of balance control, physical co-ordination and control of force lie at the foundation of good Judo. The application of the principles may vary, but the principles themselves do not change. Transference brings the technique "home" to our students. If our students can visualize and practice the application of the technique in a "real" situation, then they will be much more willing to learn the technique, because transference has provided added value to the lesson.

Meaning, Value and Benefit: If we teach techniques that build on a strong foundation and that have transference to real situations **as perceived by the students**, then it follows that what the students are learning has value and meaning to them. For instance: If you are very excited about competition but a student of yours couldn't care less about competition, then all your encouragement about how this or that drill will help your student in tournament is falling on deaf ears. The drill may have all sorts of application to your view of the world, but to the student in question, it has no meaning. Students will always learn more quickly if **they** believe that what you are teaching has value to **them**. When students have a sense of meaning and perceive value in what they are learning they will remain motivated and want to learn more. Conversely the reverse is also true. If there is no meaning in what the students are asked to do, they will lose interest and quit.

When you teach encourage questions that establish an understanding of value. Ask questions to find out whether your students actually understand what they are doing and whether or not they understand why they are doing it. Find out if what they are learning has meaning to them.

There is a second aspect to meaning, which relates to the intrinsic versus the extrinsic benefits that your students derive from the activities that you ask of them. Intrinsic benefits are those which the students create for themselves whereas extrinsic benefits are those that the students earn such as rank, competition honors, approval of parents, coaches, peers, etc..

In the final analysis, students take Judo to improve how they feel about themselves. The non-stated goal is to improve self-worth and self-confidence. If what we teach does not feed that goal, or the stated goals (fitness, security, competition etc.), then the students will lose interest and quit. As an instructor, it is important for you to know what motivates your students to come back to class and to perform at their best. By continually pushing our students' "hot buttons" we keep them invested in the process of learning. Don't just take it for granted that your students will keep coming back. Find out what it is that motivates them to come back and ensure that you continue to provide that level of meaning or those perceived benefits.

Satisfaction and Enjoyment: There is an adage, which says that success occurs when preparation meets opportunity. This means that when the opportunity is at hand (rank test, demonstration, tournament, real self-defense situation), the appropriate kinds of preparation will prevent poor performance. Having effectively prepared your students, they will feel good about themselves when they successfully use that preparation in the context of an opportunity-based situation.

In terms of teaching, your students will feel success when they have practiced a drill and can then use it effectively. This creates a win-win situation for the player and the coach as well as creating positive synergy in the class as a whole. If your students do not have success then they will experience frustration. In almost all instances, a lack of success is because you have asked your students to do something (from Martens, 1990):

> i) That is beyond their current level of physical, mental or emotional development,
> ii) Without emphasizing the key elements,
> iii) Without adequate preparation,
> iv) That is too complex and needs to be broken down further.

When your students do not experience success do not blame them. Look at yourself and what you are expecting of them. Are you being too rigid in your demands or have you missed a key ingredient necessary for the students to learn? In the final analysis, enjoyment leads to high levels of motivation and an increased desire to learn more. If your students aren't enjoying themselves, why should they come back to the next class?

Reinforcement and Feedback: As coaches, we often tend to think of reinforcement as giving praise for things we like, but there is much more to it than that. Reinforcement is associated with Operant Conditioning as described by B.F. Skinner (Klein, 2002; Ormond, 1999) and creates an increase in a behavior as a function of the consequences associated with an event. It stands to reason therefore that something, which reinforces behavior in one player, may have no effect on another player. Reinforcement events will therefore be specific to each player. There are two types of reinforcement: Positive and negative. Positive reinforcement involves any event that increases a behavior that was occurring before the event; negative reinforcement removes something aversive and results in an increase in the behavior that was occurring before the aversive event (Klein, 2002). The critical point when using feedback is that it must be immediate, specific and should create a positive outcome. Giving immediate praise when you see something you like creates an association between a behavior and a reward. Moreover it is important to be specific and to praise exactly what you liked about what you saw. Saying "Nice throw!" doesn't cut it...the student has no idea just exactly what was good about it. Tell the student that the throw had great hip position, or shoulder rotation, something.....but be specific and link it to the outcome, so that the student will know what to do again and what result will be achieved by repeating the action. Therefore in your corrections, you should explain **how** something can be improved and **why** it can be improved.

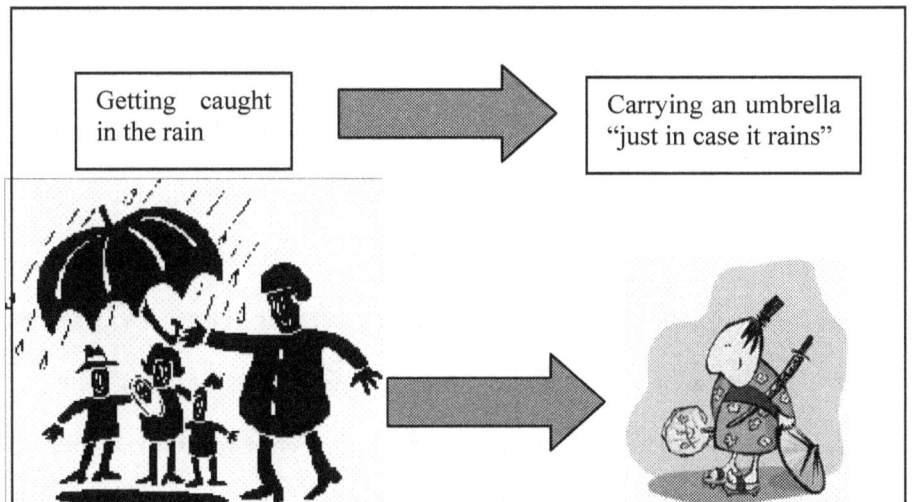

Figure 4: An excellent analogy of negative reinforcement is the "umbrella analogy" (Tony Zimkowski, Pers. Comm., 2004): A person goes out in the rain and gets wet. You give them an umbrella and they stay dry, which removes the aversive element of getting wet in the rain. The continued practice of staying dry by using an umbrella in the rain, eventually translates itself into actions like carrying an umbrella when it's cloudy outside, but not yet raining.

Make corrections to technical performance using the "Do this, don't do this, do this" formula. People tend to remember the first and last things you tell them. In correction, show and tell your students what you want, then show or tell what they are doing and then repeat what you want. Always explain why you want the change. Also, when you correct technique, sandwich correction between rewards. For instance: "Great hip position, now bring your front foot back to here, you'll get more rotation into the throw which will add power to the throw, great hip position though". You will notice that in the example we used positive reinforcement to do two things: Reinforce what we liked (the hip position) and to correct an action that would improve performance (moving the front foot back further). In another example, two players are practicing foot sweeps together and one player is getting kicked in the shin by the other player. The player getting kicked is becoming less and less willing to do foot sweeps. In this example the coach could use negative reinforcement to remove the aversive element (getting kicked in the shin) by calling for a change in partners. The coach could then speak to the player who was doing the kicking about how to improve the action without hurting his or her partners. If the player who was getting kicked returns to a behavior in which foot sweeps are being performed without anxiety, then the negative reinforcement (removing the aversive element by changing partners) was successful in increasing the behavior that was prevalent prior to the aversive event. In both cases an increase in the desired behavior is achieved.

When reinforcement is used correctly, it creates a positive outcome. Consequently when we use reinforcement in appropriate ways, we are encouraging our students to develop positive self-expectancy. When they are given positive feedback (in the form of positive or negative reinforcement), students will tend to respond with an increase in their own expectation that they can achieve personal success. With continuous, specific reinforcements, which create positive outcomes, students will internalize the notion that they are capable of success and they will expect to be successful. The result is that they will also expect more of themselves, thereby improving their intrinsic sense of self-worth. Negative feedback, however, tends to undermine self-belief and does nothing to enhance the learning environment. Unfortunately we use lines like "Don't do that" all too frequently. These sorts of phrases are coded into almost all of us from an early age, and it is easy to fall into using them when we coach our players.

Cooperation: Learning Judo requires varying levels of cooperation at different times during training. It is a critical factor of retention that the student and the instructor are aware of what is appropriate for any given drill. Obviously, when first learning a technique complete cooperation between partners is an essential requirement for ensuring safety and for learning the technique effectively. Conversely, when students are practicing randori, greater levels of resistance, noncompliance and competition are appropriate. Randori however, is not shiai. Randori is an opportunity to experiment and learn how to improve your skills in a free flowing, volatile and highly dynamic environment. It is not a license to continually blast everyone in the class with your best tournament skill. There is a time and place for intense practice, but class randori may not be the right time. Again, it is the instructor who must monitor and enforce the appropriate levels of cooperation in order to protect the safety of the players, maintain value in training, prevent frustration and minimize risk of injury. There is a fine line between competitive spirit and the loss of control in a class. The instructor carries the responsibility for ensuring that both cooperation and competitive spirit remain within specified limits.

Figure 5: When students are learning a Judo form such as Ju No Kata, high levels of cooperation are absolutely essential.

Creativity: George Weers, a former Chair of the USJA Coaching Education Committee is fond of saying "creativity lives on the edge of chaos". Students will find much more meaning in what they are learning when they have the opportunity to experiment and discover Judo for themselves. We said earlier that if you teach the principles early on, then the students will tend to invent throws that demonstrate the application of a given principle. This is creativity at it best. In any learning process the aspect of **creativity** is what makes the experience unique to each student. It is therefore important to encourage experimentation within the parameters of the lesson plan. Each student will make any action fit his or her own body and develop a "personalized form". We must avoid forcing our students into exact replicas of who we think they should be. Our students will make many mistakes along the way to creating the skills which work well for them and that is at it should be. Given that the coach provides appropriate reinforcement, his or her students will succeed through their failures. Every mistake is a precious lesson that brings us closer to the performance goal we are working to attain.

Creativity is part of learning how to master our mistakes and turn them into success. Such moments of creativity can be called "Edison moments" after the famous inventor. There is a well-known story about Edison concerning a time when a young journalist interviewed him. The journalist asked Edison why he didn't quit after so many failures at attempting to invent the light bulb. Edison replied that the young man clearly did not understand the nature of life. Edison then explained that he hadn't experienced 5000 failures, he had in fact successfully discovered 5000 ways that would not work and therefore was precisely 5000 ways closer to the way, which would work. This is not mere semantics. It is a critical ingredient in understanding the difference between those who will succeed in life and those who will quit.

As instructors it is our duty to promote creativity, to nurture it and to foster its use in our classes. Failure to do so will stifle your students. It will also limit your own potential and prevent you from seeing innovative ways of doing things.

Form and Function: Form can be defined as the shape of something or the manner in which an action occurs. It is normal to expect that form follows function, insofar as changes in form will occur to meet the specific demands of a given function.

For aspiring Judoka, form and function are intimately tied to the creation of an arsenal of defensive and offensive skills that will be both effective and efficient should tactical situations occur requiring their use. A tactical situation is one in which an opportunity exists to employ a learned skill. In Judo settings, the size, shape, speed, and direction of travel, available weapons, fitness and/or fatigue level and relative skill levels of the combatants will affect tactical situations.

When we teach Judo, we offer techniques by names such as shoulder throw, or hip throw, but every student will develop a personalized form of the techniques we teach. The essential elements of the technique will still be there, but the form will be necessarily altered to fit the age, physique and fitness level of the student as well as the tactical situations in which each student finds him or herself. Form then, is an individual thing, and if an instructor wishes to be successful it is necessary to recognize that within the prescribed limits of a technique there is a lot of room for students to evolve their own form.

In its essential truth, good form gets the job done. It may not always look very pretty, but if it does the job effectively then it has good form. Terry Kelly, a very successful Judo Coach from Santa Rosa, California and a member of the USJA Coaching Education Committee, calls this "ugly Judo." But the main point is that "good form" is both biomechanically sound and functionally efficient. Good form can therefore be defined as any technique that gets the required job (function) done effectively and efficiently. Put another way…Judo is about maximum efficiency, minimum effort.

As coaches, it is important for us also to recognize that "form" changes over time. Often changes over time are associated with proximity to a qualified instructor and with an individual's interpretation of perceived meaning. This is particularly true within the Judo kata. Different instructors will have different insights into a given "kata" and therefore teach it in their own way. As a matter of course, the form of the kata will evolve over time as successive generations of instructors get further removed from the originator of the kata. In essence, successive re-interpretation of the kata will lead to subtle changes, which will magnify over time. By way of illustration, anyone who has competed in kata competitions in either Judo or Karate knows that there is a "standard accepted" form of any specific kata. We also know that scores given at different tournaments for essentially the same "form" can vary widely according to the judges' interpretation of what constitutes the accepted standard on that day.

Final Comment: The conditions of learning are an inter-related set of conditions that creates the best possible learning environment. It is the instructor's responsibility to create the learning environment and to foster the ability of the students to acquire the best possible experience from their learning opportunities. The conditions of learning should never be far from your mind when you teach class, develop lesson plans or build a curriculum.

Having said that however, understanding and creating the appropriate conditions of learning is only the first step in the educational process. The second step is to understand how students learn, and we shall deal with this aspect of education in the next section on the psychology of learning.

II. Psychology of Learning

There is a progression to learning. When your students begin training they have no real knowledge of the nature of the task they are undertaking. At much higher levels of training there are moments in which Judoka act instinctively without ever thinking consciously about the actions being performed. The progression from beginner to expert passes through four very distinct phases of mastery. Interestingly enough, most people tend to rate themselves higher on the four levels of mastery than their abilities actually show them to be. Be that as it may, we can recognize the four levels of mastery as being:

    i)   <u>Uninformed Incompetence</u>. At this stage of development we don't know that we don't know anything. We do what feels normal or seems right or natural. We work mostly on instinct rather than any learned facts.

    ii)   <u>Informed Incompetence</u>. At this stage we are aware that we don't know anything. We also know that we have just begun to learn and that there is so much we don't know. We make frequent errors, have momentary flashes of insight and are definitely on the steep end of the learning curve.

    iii)   <u>Conscious Competence</u>. At this level we are pretty good at what we do. We know a high percentage of the curriculum; can perform the required techniques with some degree of proficiency and feel pretty good about what we have achieved. We can be relied upon to get things right and can be left alone to figure out a problem based on the information that we have already been given. Everyone who embarks on a learning journey of any kind should be able to reach this level of mastery.

iv) <u>Unconscious Competence</u>. At this level we act on instinct once again. Our knowledge is so much a part of us that we act instinctively and with a high degree of accuracy. In Judo, performance at this level is often referred to as "mushin" or "mind of no mind." Mushin occurs when the expert performs a skill without consciously planning the skill ahead of time. Early in our training, moments of mushin are sporadic and unpredictable events, but as our mastery increases so does our ability to act appropriately without conscious thought.

Figure 6: Pat Burris, Olympic Athlete and National Coach is giving a demonstration of a skill that is so much a part of him, that he is almost in a meditative state of complete relaxation as he teaches.

The journey through the four levels of mastery is controlled by many factors, not the least of which is the teaching paradigm. Since this is a section on the psychology of learning, we will not discuss the possible teaching paradigms beyond the observation that it is possible to teach from technique, principle or situation. To some extent these paradigms are mutually exclusive and how you approach them will have a major impact on the type of learning environment that you create. We will discuss teaching paradigms in Levels II and III.

From the perspective of the psychology of learning, the first thing to recognize when teaching the syllabus of Judo is that our students are often taught **techniques**. The questions we should ask however, when we develop a syllabus are:

i) **How** do our students learn and
ii) **What** do our students learn?

Certainly, when we test our students we can expect them to be able to produce a named series of "techniques" or "skills" as a demonstration of learned requirements, which presupposes that learning has taken place. We can also expect our students to perform the techniques that they learned earlier with greater efficiency than the techniques they have only recently learned, which further presupposes that progress has been made over time.

As your students progress through the four levels of mastery, they will also turn the techniques into **skills** (Gleeson, 1983). A skill is a testament to quality of the learning experience, and a technique is a tool of teaching. We practice techniques until they become useful, at which time they can be called skills.

The keys, which turn techniques into skills, are setting, practice and performance. Skill development therefore, is the litmus test of true learning. It is axiomatic that repetition in the correct setting is the mother of skill. We repeat the technique over and over, making small adjustments in the technique as we evaluate our ability to produce a desired result. By constantly monitoring practice performance, improving the quality of our repetitions and performing the technique in the setting in which it will be required, the technique evolves into a skill. A skill therefore is the external demonstration of an internalized technique. In terms of body movements, techniques tend to be choppy whereas skills are executed with grace and efficiency of movement. Consistent improvements will therefore lead to skill (Martens, 1990, NCCP, 1979). The process of learning a given technique will create a more or less permanent improvement in ability, not just in the technique being taught, but by extension, in other areas of the student's experience. There is behavioral change, which is demonstrated by the improvement in ability, but underlying that, there is also a cognitive change. Cognitive change is a change in the student's abilities with respect to his or her powers of mental association (Ormond, 1999).

So, from the perspective of this course we need to understand how our students acquire the information that will lead them through the four levels of mastery.

When learning a physical action, a student can blueprint a simple action, but the complex world of Judo requires that our students develop highly adaptable motor programs in order to successfully complete the assigned task of learning Judo. We can envision a blueprint of a simple action as something that could be transferred from the instructor to the student by visual example, and verbal instruction, followed by physical imitation (Martens, 1990). An old teaching adage states that students will remember nothing of what you say and only half of what they see. Consequently, it is critical that what we say, as instructors must be congruent with what we show. Give a good visual image backed up by a few precise words as pointers for the student to copy. The teaching method is a stimulus to the student, from which the student will derive the necessary information to build a blueprint of a simple action. There are very few whole actions in Judo, which can be blueprinted, without first breaking them down to smaller parts. An example of a simple action that can be blueprinted is the action of standing on one leg and sweeping with the other, using a wall to help maintain balance. This is a simple action that can be abstracted later into any number of possible scenarios. Once the mechanics have been blueprinted and are understood, it is easier to introduce unassisted balance back into the equation and then to add a partner. Successful "games" that are used in children's classes often rely on this principle of learning, by isolating a simple core action and thereby acting as an indispensable building block for later learning.

Complex actions, which constitute the bulk of Judo-related activities, require motor programs (Martens, 1990), which are produced when the student abstracts information from other areas of knowledge that pertain to the drill being taught. There are many "judo-like" actions that children do with innate understanding, such a tripping over a playmate in the playground, or wrestling with siblings. These aspects of physical activity can be the base from which a beginning student of Judo can abstract data necessary to build a complex motor program.

As an example: You can be given a blueprint of how to write the alphabet, you can also be taught to read and write words, but you could not possibly be taught every single word combination that is possible using the words that you have learned. To follow through the analogy, in Judo, the techniques we use are the letters, the combinations and counters are the words and effective randori or shiai performance is the skillful use of the language. Obviously, by this stage in the development of our students, behavioral modification has been dramatic and their patterns of mental association have also changed. The changes may have been so profound in fact, that when they step on the tournament mat, your students may be capable of completely novel mental associations, which you as their coach might not have predicted.

When building motor programs, the use of B.F. Skinner's approach is one of the most effective ways of obtaining the best results from your students. According to Ormond (1999), Skinner's approach (also called Operant Conditioning) requires that drill practice should be supported by performance goals, clear guidance, and **immediate, constructive** feedback provided by the instructor. When students perform their drills, provide reinforcement of the actions you want to increase. A direct result of the reinforcement is that the likelihood of the behavior being repeated is enhanced (emphasizes a desirable action). Positive reinforcement will add something to the training environment (for instance: Specific praise) that leads to an increase in the frequency of desired outcomes. When actions occur that create unwanted outcomes, it is important to use negative reinforcement. Negative reinforcement takes away the aversive element from the situation (for instance: A painful experience every time a drill is practiced). In both cases the result will be constructive improvement in performance.

It is clear therefore, that students will take the information that they have been given, modify it, abstract it and recombine it with other data to make it useful for any situation in which they will use the skill. Any time students use a skill they need five pieces of information (modified from Martens, 1990):

i) The environmental conditions in which the skill will be applied.
ii) The kinetic demands of the skill such as speed, force, direction etc..
iii) The actual consequences of the action.
iv) A comparison of the actual outcome with the intended outcome.
v) An awareness of how to modify the motor program to achieve the desired result.

You will notice that much of this information has little to do with the actual technique so much as the environment and situation in which it is being used. It is clear then, that learning must occur at both a physical (behavioral) and a mental (cognitive) level and must lead to an awareness by the student that he or she has the ability to abstract data from a variety of sources.

In the next stage of our investigation of the way in which students learn, we need to understand that as we progress from technique to skill in the four levels of mastery, students will also go through three stages of learning, which involve a mental stage, a physical stage and an automatic stage.

In the early stages of learning, students will use their mental capabilities to understand what is required to perform the desired technique. In the middle stage, students will spend time with physical practice, learning the fundamental movements and refining the motor program according to the mistakes that define the boundaries of successful execution. The quality of feedback during the practice stage is critical. Students gain sensory feedback from each performance as well as verbal and non-verbal feedback from their instructors. The rate of progress at this stage is therefore often dependent upon the quality of the communication between instructor and student. In the later stages of learning, the performance becomes automatic. At this stage students will tend to correct errors almost instinctively and thinking about what they are doing will actually hurt their performance (Martens, 1990).

To summarize, at this point we understand that students will progress through three stages of learning any given action and will move from a condition of uninformed incompetence to unconscious competence as they progress through the four levels of mastery.

The question now becomes, how exactly do your students learn? We do not all learn things in the same way so we need to understand that apart from the stages of learning, there are also ways of learning.

Students are visual, auditory or kinesthetic learners. Visually oriented students like to see lots of demonstrations of techniques, whereas auditory learners prefer to hear explanations and talk things out. Kinesthetically motivated students will understand by doing repetitions of the technique and will often try to physically follow along as the instructor demonstrates a new technique. It becomes important for the instructor to touch all the learning styles during the teaching presentation and to understand the differences between the three approaches to learning and the specific needs that each type of student will have in order to learn effectively (Martens, 1990).

As well as differing ways of acquiring information, students also have different ways of processing the data they receive. There are at least four ways in which students respond to, and process data:

    i)   Global thinkers or Analytical thinkers. Global thinkers will see the big picture and like to be shown the application of what they do to other areas of their knowledge. Analytic thinkers will break things down to understand how they work. If you use kata (practice of form) as an example, global thinkers will want to be shown the whole thing, whereas analytical thinkers will tend to process each part of the kata separately until they can build a cohesive whole. Global thinkers will get the whole form and then work on perfecting it.

    ii)   Similarity-based thinkers versus Difference-based thinkers. Similarity-based thinkers will tend to process information according to how closely it matches what they already know, whereas difference-based thinkers will tend to see the differences between what they know and what you are teaching. Similarity-based thinkers will see the common elements between techniques and difference-based thinkers will see what separates the techniques into categories. Similarity versus difference-based thinking is more a matter of degree to which your students demonstrate a tendency, rather than a black and white process.

iii) Pleasure seekers versus Pain evaders. These people respond in terms of benefits versus costs. Pleasure seekers will be motivated to perform because of what they stand to gain from doing something, whereas pain evaders will be motivated by what they stand to lose if they don't do something (Robbins, 1986). As an example of this pleasure-seeking tournament players will be motivated to perform repetitions of a drill because they might be better to able to win a match. In contrast, pain-avoiders will be motivated to perform the repetitions because if they don't acquire the skill, they might lose more matches.

iv) Internally referenced versus externally referenced thinkers. Internally referenced thinkers have a very strong self-image and belief system and will monitor their performance according to the progress that they have made over time. Externally based people will tend to compare themselves to those around them and seek outside approval that what they are doing meets the established criteria of performance. Internally referenced people will tend to get frustrated if they do not feel themselves to be making the progress that they believe they should be making. Conversely, externally referenced people will tend to get frustrated if they perceive that people who are at the same level as themselves are making more progress. From a coaching perspective, you should encourage internal referencing, especially if you deal with competitors. A person with a healthy internal referencing attitude will tend to accept the inevitable ups and downs of competition with ease, provided that they can see that they are improving their performance regardless of the outcome of any given match. A person who uses external referencing will not weather these challenges so easily. Internal referencing students with a healthy attitude who face a losing slump will tend to look within themselves for a solution, whereas the external referencing students will tend to look for outside causes for the problem.

When we coach students we tend to teach in one of two ways. We either teach the way we were taught or the way we learn best, but it is clear that a good instructor must learn how to present the same information in differing ways to different groups of students, so that they can all learn effectively. One of the teaching goals of the Judo instructor should be to assist and encourage students to step outside of their normal learning or processing modes. When we do this, we can often create opportunities for periods of insight and rapid growth. Seeing things in a new light can often lead to moments of insight that have large-scale trickle down effects throughout the student's awareness.

III. Safety in the Dojo

In this section we shall examine your responsibilities as a coach and also look at how you can reduce the risk of injury through the use of simple protocols. We will also look at three specific components of training that impact overall safety and which can further reduce risk of injury, namely the warm-up, the use of stretching protocols and the cool-down.

General Safety Considerations: Almost all authorities recognize that the safety of your players is the primary responsibility of the coach (Corcoran and Graden, 1998; Flegel, 1992; Judo Canada, 1983; Martens, 1990; Mitchell, 1988; NCCP, 1979). Much of the material in this section is gleaned from these sources. While it is true that it is the personal responsibility of the students to monitor their own performance, they rely upon the coach to tell them what new techniques they are capable of performing and what techniques they are ready to learn. If students are asked to learn something for which they do not feel ready, they will feel confused and frustrated. Their lack of preparedness and understanding will also lead to a higher risk of injury. Ultimately, if you ask your players to do something for which they do not feel prepared you will invite an erosion of trust and respect combined with a loss of confidence in your ability to teach or to understand their needs.

As a coach you have several duties, which deal with issues of safety and negligence. Many of these duties are self-evident, but it is good for you to keep them in the front of your mind when you consider what you are teaching and the methods you use. These duties relate to the nature of teaching, the teaching environment and how you prepare yourself to fulfill the role of coach. Let's look at the nature of the teaching first:

i) Teach from a lesson plan. Plan the activity and have written lesson plans as an integral part of the overall learning program. Keep a written record of all lesson plans. We will discuss this in Levels II & III

ii) Provide clear and precise instruction using appropriate pedagogical methods for the age, maturity level, skill level, fitness level and rank of your classes. We will discuss this a lot more in Levels III & IV.

iii) Make sure that your players are reasonably matched for experience, size, age, or gender as appropriate. The applications to age- and gender-appropriate training are obvious, but it also applies to training competitors versus non-competitors. If your players are unmatched for any reason, there is a much higher risk of injury. This is especially true when high-ranking students are doing randori with lower ranked students and when smaller, weaker students are working with larger, stronger students.

iv) Explain the appropriate levels of cooperation and contact and enforce them during class. As a coach you need to be ever vigilant for the use of strength and ego in class practice. The inappropriate use of either is inevitably going to result in injury. Be willing to act swiftly to stop the overt use of strength in unwarranted situations and stop excesses of ego immediately.

v) Understand and recognize the occurrence of an injury. Know also how to evaluate the level and severity of an injury once it has occurred. There are many occasions when a student can shake off a slight physical trauma and can continue training. There are other times when trauma means that an injury has occurred and at such times it is much better to advise a student to sit out a class, rather than risk turning a mild acute injury into a much more serious acute or even chronic injury. Clear communication between coach and student are essential in the evaluation of an injury. There are very few settings in which inattention to an injury is the right course of action. We might argue that a medal match at the Olympics might qualify, but that is between the coach and the player. Conversely, a regularly scheduled class practice is not the time to ignore injury. We can always recover if we are hurt and come back to class later, but if we ignore an injury and continue to train we can do long-term damage that will be harder, or perhaps, impossible to repair. For a discussion of common injuries in the martial arts, refer to Estwanik (1996). We will look at this area of responsibility in more detail in Level III.

vi) Evaluate students for inability to participate. Understand that signs of fatigue, injury, frustration, lack of concentration or lack of control are pre-incident indicators of high-risk situations. Always act swiftly to reduce risk. Monitor in-class performance, checking for confusion, frustration and fatigue. Allow your students to rest when they need to and allow free access to water at any time during practice. Students who are experiencing both frustration and fatigue may need both a rest and a simpler task. In these circumstances it might not be appropriate to break down a drill for the whole class, but a single student might benefit from being given a simpler drill if he or she is experiencing frustration. Remember when you have a group of mixed ranks doing the same drill, that novice players with a lower level of fitness will be placing much more stress on their bodies than mid-ranked players who are beginning to make impressive gains in physical fitness. Make sure that your non-verbal and verbal expectations, as well as the use of appropriate positive and negative reinforcements, are consistent with encouraging your novice players to evaluate their own performance and to do their very best. Having said that, however, you should remind your novice players to live within their own limits. Seek clarification so as to lessen the likelihood of confusion and frustration.

vii) As an instructor you should warn of risks often. Warn of risks that are general in nature and also warn of specific concerns when introducing new materials. Make sure that you tell the students about risks when applying joint locks and chokes. Discuss the limits of "safe" play and discuss the ways in which risk factors may be reduced. Sometimes all that is needed is a gentle reminder to your students to maintain control and be considerate of their training partners.

viii) Provide appropriate emergency supplies and assistance. Unless you are a medical professional, you are not qualified to provide medical assistance beyond following simple, expected first aid procedures. We will examine this area in more detail in the next section and again in Level III

ix) Avoid turning your back to the mat. Keep a clear view of as much of the training area as possible at all times.

x) Never leave the training area without a certified, assistant instructor in your place who understands and can continue your lesson plan.

There are safety factors that pertain to the environment in which you teach. We do not always get to control all aspects of our training facility, especially if we are renting space in some multi-purpose facility such as a school, YMCA, or church. Having said that, however, you can ensure the following:

i) Provide a safe training environment. Check for hard objects, loose pictures, trophies that may fall on your players, or protruding objects with which your players may collide during practice. Make sure that there is an adequate safety area around the mat, even during regular training (not just in competition). Moreover, make sure that you provide adequate space so as to enable everyone to work with minimal risk of collision. Of equal importance is the unrestricted mingling of different weight groups during training. As an example imagine the possible liability that you could create if a pair of heavyweight students happened to lose balance and fall into a pair of your lightweight women who just happened to be in the same area of the mat at the moment of the incident. If your mat space is limited, you may have to put a cap on class size or use a practice rotation to control the number of participants on the mat at any one time.

ii) Provide and maintain adequate training equipment. Be particularly sensitive to the nature of the falling surface and crash pads. Paying attention to the surface upon which your players are moving and falling can prevent a lot of knee injuries and broken toes. Moreover, make sure that there is adequate cushioning to prevent injuries to the shoulders, elbows and back when falling. If possible, the training surface should be spring-loaded. This goes a long way towards minimizing injuries and has been a standard practice in the gymnastics industry for years.

A distinctly separate group of actions are those that occur before anyone even steps onto the mat. These actions should become part of your standard operating procedure. By taking some simple precautions before class, the instructor can do much to improve safety of the training environment. Attention to these details sends very clear messages to your students about your training values, such as long-term investment versus short-term gain. The students who feel that safety is a very real concern to the coach will be much more apt to work harder and take greater risks. The logic behind this statement is that the students know that they have entered a partnership with their coach in which they are both cognizant of the levels of risk and safety of the training environment. Judo is all about risk; there is no getting away from it. Anytime you give your body to someone else for them to throw onto the planet, you are taking a risk. The players who know that they are taking these risks in a safe environment are going to be more relaxed, calm and considerate of their fellows. Accordingly, the things that a coach needs to do before any player steps on the mat include:

i) Have every new student read and sign a "Warning, waiver, release of liability, assumption of risk and agreement to participate" form (written by Scott Conway for the American Council on the Martial Arts Instructors Course, used herein by permission of the National Association of Professional Artists. See Appendices).

ii) Have every new student fill out a health history when he or she enrolls (see Appendices).

iii) Give copies of the class safety rules, and blood policy to every student when they enroll. If the student is a minor, go over the safety rules, etiquette and blood policy with the parent and make sure they also go over the rules with the child.

iv) Have a fully stocked first aid kit on hand (Flegel, 1992).

v) Be CPR certified and take a first aid course.

vi) Police the training area, changing rooms and restrooms before practice for possible hazards.

vii) Teach from a syllabus and prepare lesson plans in advance.

Most of these safety issues are straightforward and stem from a clear understanding of your primary responsibility as a coach. Never lose sight of the fact that what you do, how you do it and where you do it, will always be measured against your obligation to ensure the safety of your players.

In the next section we will examine some specific areas of safety in the dojo. Specifically, how we conduct warm-ups, stretching activities and a cool-down.

The Warm-up: The warm-up is an indispensable part of reducing the likelihood of injury in class (Byl, 2004; Corcoran and Graden, 1998; Martens, 1990; Mitchell, 1988, NCCP, 1979; Powers and Howley, 1990). A thorough warm-up allows the student to become both psychologically and physiologically prepared for the more intense activities to follow. As such the warm-up bridges the gap between coming to class and doing the work expected in the lesson plan to be presented. One of the most important aspects of doing a warm-up is that it increases the state of psychological arousal by inducing the secretion of endorphins that stimulate the body to perform at a higher level. A warm-up should be a whole-body experience, using all the muscles that will be used during the class (Byl, 2004). Warm-ups should include range of motion exercises as well as cardiovascular and mild stretching components but should be tailored to the fitness level and age of the students. Warm-ups should be rhythmic and be accompanied by activities that emphasize the full range of movement for all joints that will be used in the practice. Excellent warm-up drills include lower intensity versions of movements that you will use later in class.

Figure 7: Using a footwork drill as part of a warm-up at the All Carolina Camp. The emphasis of the drill is to reduce members in the circle by taking out their feet. This warm-up drill is a lot of fun, requires balance, teamwork and strategy. Notice how the groups are matched for size and age. Notice also the body language of the senior instructor (leaning toward the group) giving personal attention to the younger group at the rear.

It is very important to develop a wide range of warm-up exercises, so that you can vary the warm-up procedure over time. All too often we fall into the trap of using the same warm-up exercises repeatedly. By varying the warm-up, instructors are able to minimize the level to which the warm-up loses its efficacy because the student's minds and bodies have adapted to the drills used in the warm-up. By varying the warm-ups, students will remain motivated, their bodies will not fall into a "warm-up comfort zone" and the students will continue to derive both psychological and physiological benefits from the warm-up itself.

Warm-ups also act as a good transition between out-of-class activities and the in-class concentration required for excellence in Judo. The reasoning behind this statement is that warm-ups can be a good time for the students to indulge in relaxation (stress release), focusing, meditation and/or visualization.

If your players have received an adequate warm-up the physical and mental preparation for class will inevitably lead to a reduction in the risk of injury which will, in turn, promote better technical accomplishments and a more relaxed and enjoyable training environment.

In summary then a warm-up should:

i) Build fundamental psychomotor skills
ii) Involve large body actions using full range of motion exercises
iii) Use body movements that simulate actions that will be required in the lesson plan
iv) Elevate core and muscle temperature
v) Increase heart rate
vi) Increase breathing rate
vii) Increase circulation of blood to the muscles
viii) Stimulate joint lubrication
ix) Include a mild stretching component, once the body is warm
x) Stimulate endorphin release for optimal arousal
xi) Stimulate psychological arousal ensuring the players are mentally motivated, prepared and focused on the class ahead.

Stretching: We will examine stretching as a separate unit because there are many misconceptions about when and how to do any stretching. The purpose of stretching is to increase the range of motion for a particular joint; this presupposes that the joint we wish to stretch is well lubricated and relaxed, i.e. warm. Since the structure of the joint is a limiting factor, the only things that we can change are the elasticity (or lack thereof) of the muscles, tendons and ligaments surrounding the joints. Muscles work the joint, tendons attach the muscles to the bones and ligaments join bone to bone across the joint. Muscles and tendons are elastic, which means that if they are stretched they can return to their original size when the stretching force is removed. Ligaments are non-elastic, but can be stretched, which means that they do not return to their original length once the stretching force has been removed. In any joint there are two sets of muscles used for flexing and extending the joint. The two-muscle sets work as a pair and are known as the agonist and antagonist muscles (Luttgens and Wells, 1989). When the agonist muscle is contracting and shortening it changes the joint angle, and the antagonist muscle on the other side of the joint must relax and lengthen or else the two sets of muscles will be working against each other. Flexion involves decreasing the joint angle, and extension involves increasing the joint angle.

We can recognize three types of stretching:

    i) One of the very best forms of stretching exercise is called proprioceptive neuromuscular facilitation (P.N.F.). Stretching using P.N.F. involves holding a muscular contraction followed by relaxing the muscle and allowing it to stretch, then repeating the cycle (Anderson, and Anderson, 2000;

Estwanik, 1996; Luttgens and Wells, 1989). P.N.F. stretching therefore involves four stages: 1. Flexion of the joint to develop relaxed muscular stretch, 2. Resisted muscular contraction for a slow count of ten, 3. Increase in relaxed flexion, 4. Repetition of the cycle three times. P.N.F. stretches can be done on your own, but also work very well when you have a partner who cooperates fully with you during the exercise. Since both people are working together, P.N.F. stretching is an excellent way of cooling down a class both physiologically and psychologically.

Figure 8: P.N.F. Stretching is a great way to cool down at the end of class.

ii) Static Stretching involves holding a slow, smooth stretching action. During a static stretch one set of muscles (agonist) is used to stretch the opposite muscles (antagonist) on the same joint (Anderson and Anderson, 2000). For instance, an example of a static stretch involves using a contraction of the quadriceps muscles of the thigh to stretch a relaxed hamstring muscle on the opposite side of the leg. In "static active" stretching a person stretches a set of muscles without a partner to help them. In the "static passive" stretch, a partner assists and provides extra "push" into the stretch (Luttgens and Wells, 1989). Static passive stretching is not always a good idea because the partner is the person who is controlling the force of the stretch.

iii) Ballistic. Ballistic stretching involves bouncing during the stretch. This type of stretching is very bad and results in a reflex muscle contraction, which can lead to high incidences of injury (Estwanik, 1996). The muscle stretch reflex is an automatic muscular contraction that occurs whenever your muscles are stretched too far or during ballistic (bouncing) types of stretches.

A warm-up combined with mild stretching before a vigorous work out reduces the risk of injury and increases the range of movement for the joints (Corcoran and Graden, 1998; Judo Canada, 1983; Mitchell, 1988, NCCP, 1979). It is important to recognize that stretching is not a warm-up in itself, but that once the body temperature, heart rate and blood circulation rate have been elevated, stretching can be used as part of a warm-up (Anderson and Anderson, 2000; Herbert and Gabriel, 2002). The point here is that extensive stretching should not be a big part of the warm-up. Stretching can however, be used to augment range of motion warm-up exercises. It is the warm-up that reduces the risk of injury, not the stretch.

Stretching should not feel painful, but should be taken to the point of discomfort. Pain tells you that your body is not happy with what you are expecting it to do. Each stretch should be held for about 10 seconds at the full range of stretch, followed by a ten second relaxation and a repeated stretch (Anderson and Anderson, 2000; Corcoran and Graden, 1998). Estwanik (1996) recommends that for actual lengthening of muscle and tendon fibers, three to five repetitions of a thirty-second stretch in a relaxed maximally lengthened position are required. Stretching should be smooth and steady and can involve resistance or non-resistance.

When doing mild stretching in preparation for a Judo class, it is important to emphasize range of motion exercises for the ankles, calf muscles, the quadriceps, hamstrings, hip adductors, lower and upper back, sides, shoulders, fingers and wrists. Stretching is also good after a class as a cooling down activity. In either case, move from large muscle groups to small muscle groups and work methodically through the whole body.

Cool-down: The cool-down is a mechanism by which our students reduce their state of arousal and also bring physiological parameters such as breathing and heart rate back down to normal levels. Although it should be obvious that to suddenly stop working can lead to increased risk of injury, we also need to consider the benefits of a cool-down:

    i)   Physiological: It is the physiological aspects of the cool-down that are of primary significance in our examination of safety. The obvious physiological benefits of a cool-down are in returning heart rate, blood pressure, breathing and core temperature to normal levels as well as the removal of metabolic waste products from their sites of production. A sudden stop in activity can lead to increased health-risk factors, whereas cooling the system down and allowing the body to gradually return to more normal levels of activity, places less strain on the heart and lungs and related (circulatory) systems. When the body is highly active, about 80% of the available cardiac output is being pumped to the big muscles groups, which means that less than 20% is going to the visceral organs and the brain. In actual fact, although the brain only receives 3-4% of the available cardiac output during physical activity, the absolute amount of blood going to the brain goes up slightly because the heart rate has increased. When you stop activity, the blood can pool in the muscles and needs to be redirected to normal flow patterns. If the blood is allowed to pool in the muscles then the percentage of the **available** cardiac output going to the brain may go back to about 15%, but the absolute volume of blood drops because heart rate has declined and less blood is being pumped through the heart. Failure to redirect blood flow to normal patterns can therefore cause fainting because of blood pooling in large muscle groups such as the legs. (Corcoran and Graden, 1998; Powers and Howley, 1990).

Moreover, intense physical activity burns metabolic materials in the muscles and produces metabolic waste. When student activity stops the waste products can also pool in the muscles and cause cramping or muscle soreness, unless they are flushed out of the system by less intense forms of activity.

If you want to do a stretching component in your activities, the cool-down is a good time to do it, because the muscles are already warm and the joints are well lubricated. A stretching cool-down is a good way to enhance venous return, promote waste removal as well as remove muscular tension. Consequently, a stretching component to the cool-down can enhance the overall psychological state of relaxation after intense effort as well as promote physiological well-being.

ii) <u>Psychological</u>: Although not critical to safety in the dojo, we will touch briefly upon the importance of the psychological aspects of the cool-down. If a cool-down is not employed as an integral part of the lesson plan, the cessation of intense and rewarding physical activity can marred by a sense of disappointment rather than a sense of euphoria and enthusiasm. When we are physically active the release of endorphins raises our level of arousal. If we have to stop what we are doing without a cool-down, those same endorphins are still cruising through the body and we are eager to keep going. So without a cool down, instead of feeling good when we leave class, we actually leave class feeling a sense of disappointment.

IV. Legal Considerations

It is a fact of life that we live in a litigious society, and as coaches we would be well advised to understand our legal responsibilities. The intent of the material in this section is to inform, rather than create a set of rigid standards or requirements. Most of us consider ourselves to be reasonable, prudent coaches who use common sense and who are concerned about the safety of our players. The information in this section is therefore provided to help you protect yourself. Much of what is written here comes from the ASEP Leader Course (Martens, 1990), the ACMA Coaching Course (Corcoran and Graden, 1998) and associated readings. The ASEP course was written for coaches of all sports and the ACMA manual was written for all martial artists.

Our goal is not to help you win a lawsuit; our goal is to help you avoid ever being involved in one. If this manual can provide a framework which you can use to reduce risk and which encourages you to keep records, then it will have served its purpose. The goal of this section remains the same as the rest of the manual: To have as many people doing Judo as possible, in the safest environment possible, with the greatest amount of benefit possible. The nature of doing Judo involves risk, and if we are honest, something about that appeals to us, but we can and should minimize risk from other sources. Much of what follows comes down to two things:

    i)   Reducing risks, and
    ii)   Keeping records.

Beyond your simple obligations to ensure the safety of your students, there are also legal responsibilities, which you assume the moment you choose to become a Judo coach. Ignorance of your legal responsibilities is not acceptable as an excuse, so it is a good idea to know what you are undertaking, from a legal perspective. It is also a good idea to have a working knowledge of the statutes that apply in your state, county or town. What we will discuss are generally accepted standards of legal responsibility.

Our main considerations in this section revolve around "risk management", which is why this section follows hard on the heels of the section on safety. Remember that your prime responsibility as a coach is the safety of your players. On the other hand, your prime responsibility to yourself is to keep records that attest to the fact that you do indeed view your prime responsibility as a coach as being the safety of your players. Keep adequate records of lesson plans, student forms, health history, injury reports and equipment replacement dates. These things are all part of being professional about what you do as a coach. Do not accept the argument that "I don't have time to keep all those records. I've never been sued, and I've been teaching for years...why start now?" If you are not willing to keep adequate records to protect yourself, what assurances can you offer that you are willing to protect your students?

There are four main areas that you need to be aware of: Discrimination, harassment and abuse, and negligence.

Discrimination: Discrimination is related to three aspects of coaching.

        i)   How you recruit and accept students into your classes

ii) How you promote your students

iii) Requirements of training/participation

If you refuse to accept a student for anything other than objective reasons, then you are leaving yourself open to accusations of discriminatory practices.

The process of promoting one student *over* another is in itself an act of a discriminatory nature, but that does not make it illegal. It is part of what you are expected to do as a coach. It is your judgment based upon objective reasoning that causes you to promote one student at a faster/slower rate than another. Here again, record keeping and teaching from a syllabus with testing dates can be of benefit to you. We will look at this in much more detail in Level II. Understand however, that if you hold a student back without good reason, you may have a disgruntled student and/or parent with whom you will need to deal.

The participation requirements of what we do in Judo can sometimes be misconstrued and be taken out of context. For this reason, it is your responsibility to maintain open lines of communication with parents and participants and offer the option of non-participation in a particular aspect of the training. Forcing students to do something that they do not want to do can be viewed by those students as discriminatory.

In almost all cases an open mind, open communication and record keeping will help you avoid being accused of discriminatory practices.

Harassment and abuse: The close physical nature of Judo raises the likelihood of inadvertent and accidental contact with sexually sensitive areas of the body, which in turn increases the possibility of perceived sexual harassment (same gender or mixed gender). Harassment, however, is not simply confined to issues of sexual harassment through inappropriate physical touching. Harassment could be defined as anything that makes a person feel harassed. This may seem simple and non-sensible to you, but be aware that what you may view as normal someone else might view as harassment. The point here is not what you think, but what the other person **feels**.

We offer some guidelines as to what might be considered harassment:

- Making derogatory comments about a person or group
- Making jokes or using obscene language, slurs and stories that have the purpose of demeaning or stereotyping a person or group
- The use of physical gestures that demean, degrade or show hostility towards a person or group
- Physical actions that might threaten or intimidate a person because of his or her membership in a particular group
- Leering or staring at a person because of his or her membership in a particular group

As we have just said, a large component of Judo involves grappling and it is inevitable that various and sundry body parts will be contacted during the process. The possibility of *unintentional* contact with sexually sensitive body areas or areas of the body that might be considered to be culturally off-limits by members of some groups is therefore relatively high. The possibility of a charge of molestation (of a child) or harassment (of an adult) is therefore very real. It is important for you to realize that as a coach in a supervisory position, you can be held liable for allowing a harassing or abusive environment to exist. Tolerating any of the actions listed above could be a basis for legal action because you have an affirmative duty to address the issue. In addition, coaches are responsible for the education of their staff and the development of some reporting process whereby issues of harassment can be addressed.

The solution is simple and obvious: **As a coach, be professional and enforce a similar level of performance from your players.**

Another aspect of harassment is the potential for abuse of the "power" position. As coach, you are in a position of power and under-ranking students will tend to obey your instructions because they trust and respect you and because they feel that it is a necessary part of obtaining the benefits they seek from your tutelage. You must discharge this office with complete professionalism at all times. Your students and assistants will model your example, and the risk of being accused of unwarranted activity will be lessened.

One last aspect of harassment is dealt with in the nature of the Risk Agreement (See Appendix 3). The risk agreement (Appendix 3) was developed by Scott Conway, an attorney, writing in the American Council on Martial Arts Instructor Certification Manual for the National Association of Professional Martial Artists (Corcoran and Graden, 1998) and is used herein by permission. In the Risk Agreement, we are notifying our students of the types of physical contact that will be involved and obtaining their consent. We are also offering a non-participation clause as a way of further reducing risk. From this perspective you can see why it is so important to have written documentation of informed consent in every student's file. In the case of minors, have their parents sign the forms.

Child Abuse: Although Judo practice (but not competition) is a co-ed activity, mixing age groups (children and adults) together in the same class at the same time, with the same instructor and the same lesson plan is not a good idea. If your time/space constraints are such that you have different age populations on the mat at the same time, then use assistant instructors, keep your age groups separated from each other and provide age-appropriate instruction to each group. We will talk a lot about this from a pedagogic perspective in Levels II, III and IV, but for now let us understand that keeping children out of your adult classes is simply good risk management. As an adjunct to mixed age groups, be sensitive to the risks of having adults and children changing in the same facility at the same time. Again, avoidance is simply good risk management. If there is no opportunity for child molestation, the problem will not arise. If you behave as a professional and expect your assistants to model your behavior and example, then risks in this area will be minimal.

It is a sad fact that child abuse occurs and as Judo instructors we should be on the front line protecting the lives of our young students. Child abuse can take many forms extending from physical and emotional maltreatment to sexual abuse. Sexual abuse of a child involves activities, which are designed to give sexual gratification to an adult or someone who is four years older than the victim (Block and Reece, 2005). The Boy Scouts of America manual (1998), gives a succinct definition of child abuse or neglect as involving "either the action or lack of action of a person who occupies a situation of responsibility for the care of the child". Judo instructors fall into that group.

The sexual molestation of a child often involves bribery, threats or force to coerce a child into compliance with a sexual activity. Such activity might include exhibitionism (exposure of sexually sensitive areas of the body), voyeurism (watching sexual activity), fondling (inappropriate touching) and rape. It is important to recognize that boys and girls can be sexually abused by adults or by other children. Unfortunately victims often feel shamed, humiliated, embarrassed and unable to talk about their experiences, sometimes as a direct result of the fear they feel of the molester. Victims may also be reticent to speak of their experiences because they may assume a level of personal responsibility for the abuse or fear the repercussions or anger of their parents or teachers. Molestation occurs from the abuse of positions of trust and more than 80% of sexually abused boys get abused by people they trust outside of their immediate family. However, again according to the Boy Scouts of America manual (1998), apart from the sexual abuse of boys, most abuse occurs within families. Recognizing the occurrence of sexual abuse can be difficult, especially if the child is unwilling to talk about his or her experiences.

As coaches, it is our responsibility to protect children and to teach them to "Recognize, Resist and Report" (Boy Scouts of America, 1998) instances of abuse. Equally, it is incumbent upon the coach to recognize signs of possible abuse and report such signs to the appropriate authorities. The hardest part of the 3R's is giving children the freedom to speak out when they feel they have been abused. As we have said, children are often reluctant to talk about their experiences. Judo coaches should be role models with whom the children should feel comfortable and safe. The implication of the foregoing is that children should feel that they could turn to their Judo coach for help and assistance.

If we remember that our goal is to provide safe and enjoyable, rewarding experiences for our children, it becomes incumbent upon every coach to ensure that children train in an environment that is safe, secure and free from threat. Young people are entitled to protection from abuse and instructors owe them a high level of duty in this regard. The USJA is committed to the development and implementation of policies that safeguard children, educate instructors and which create environments where "mutual benefit and welfare" exists for all who participate. In order to protect the children in our classes and our instructors we recommend the following practices when dealing with children. Our guidelines are drawn from several sources including Amateur Rowing Association (2002), Boy Scouts of America (1998), British Judo Association (NGB for judo in England) (2003), Bushido Zazen International Society (2003), English Karate Association (NGB for karate in England) (2004), Football Association of the United Kingdom (2001), YMCA (2001):

- Generate a child protection policy and hand it to every parent when a child enrolls in your program.
- Educate your instructors and all volunteers who come into contact with children in your classes concerning child safety policies.
- Instructors should communicate regularly with parents and involve them in decision-making processes that affect their children.
- Instructors should recognize that children have individual rights and treat all children with respect and dignity.

- Instructors should exhibit the highest standards of professional behavior and care at all times.
- Instructors should respect all children's touch boundaries and their rights not to be touched in ways that make them feel uncomfortable. Instructors should respect the rights of children to say "no." The use of a risk agreement, such as found in Appendix 3, which includes a non-participation clause is very helpful in creating an awareness of the expected range of physical contact involved in Judo both for the parents and the children, and clearly explains a participant's right to exclude him or herself for any activity with which he or she feels uncomfortable.
- Instructors should teach and treat all children equally.
- Instructors should encourage children to take responsibility for their own actions and decision-making. Children who feel that they are able to make decisions for themselves are much more likely to actively resist abuse and report such events to responsible adults
- Instructors should never leave children unsupervised.
- Instructors should not be alone with children and should endeavor to create settings where instructors are clearly visible to each other or other adults when they are working with children.
- Instructors should be aware of situations that can be misconstrued or manipulated by others. Examples of such situations might include being alone with the children or the use of martial arts techniques that might be easily misconstrued by onlookers.
- Instructors should check the children in class and be aware of any sign of injury or abuse and be ready to discuss their findings with a child's parents in a non-threatening manner.
- Instructors should not abuse children in any way, which includes all forms of physical (striking, shaking), verbal (humiliating, degrading),

sexual (inappropriate touching or verbal exchange) or mental (shaming, being cruel) abuse.
- Instructors should ensure that restroom facilities are unoccupied by suspicious or unknown people before allowing children to use the facilities and stand in the doorway while children are using the facilities.
- If children must be supervised in restrooms or changing areas, always ensure that instructors, parents and or officials work in pairs.
- Instructors should use age-appropriate teaching methods and maintain reasonable child/adult ratios in class. The YMCA (2002) suggests that there should be a 1:8 instructor to child ratio for children between the ages of 6 and 18. This ratio is a guideline only, because each State will have its own guidelines for childcare.
- Instructors should not engage in horse play with children
- Instructors should not allow children to use inappropriate language or behaviors unchallenged
- Instructors should not allow any child to leave class with anyone other than the child's parent, guardian or person for whom the parents have given express and written permission.
- Instructors should not take children alone in their personal vehicles, without the express permission of the child's parent.
- Never take children to your home without their parents or guardians present.
- Instructors should avoid sharing a room with children when away from home on a tournament or clinic trip without another parent or adult being present.
- Instructors should be ready to report and concerns that pertain to child protection to appropriate authorities. Appropriate authorities might include the management personnel of the church, school or YMCA facilities in which the Judo club practices, the Social Services

Department and possibly the police. It is paramount that the instructor keeps factual, written records of concern along with dates and times.

To help instructors recognize and act upon instances of potential physical and/or sexual abuse there are signs that can be helpful, such as:

- An unwillingness of a child to interact with a particular person for no obvious reason,
- Unexplainable changes in behavior such as becoming very quiet or withdrawn,
- Sudden and unexplainable mistrust of adults,
- Body language involving shying away and cowering,
- Exhibiting behaviors with sexual overtones that a child of his or her age would not normally exhibit,
- Physical evidence that sexual activity has occurred. Such evidence may include soreness, irritation or bruising of sexually sensitive areas of the body,
- Evidence that physical abuse has occurred such as bruising, scratching, cuts, burns and/or bite marks. Bruising in areas of the body that would not normally get bruised during accidental activity are warning signs, and
- Evidence of an injury for which the explanation does not seem consistent.

Other lines of evidence that indicate stress in a child's life can include:

- Self-destructive behaviors including substance abuse, self-inflicted injury, depression, thoughts or actions pertaining to suicide,
- Raised levels of personal anxiety as indicated by loss of appetite or sleep,

- Regression to earlier levels of development as evidenced by thumb sucking or bed wetting, and
- A sudden drop in academic performance, missing school or discipline problems in class.

If an instructor receives a report from a child or adult or sees clear evidence of child abuse there are several things that the instructor will need to do:

- Remember that you are not a therapist.
- Stay calm.
- Talk to the child and reinforce the fact that the child is not responsible or to blame for what happened.
- Reinforce the child's right to speak about what happened.
- Take what the child says seriously. Listen.
- Do not badger the child for details.
- Do not ask any leading questions because they might contaminate the child's testimony at a later date.
- Keep a written record including names of people involved, times, dates, locations, physical signs, dialog and other relevant information.
- Reassure the child, but do not promise to keep the matter secret. Explain to the child that it may be necessary to inform other people.
- Report the event to the appropriate authorities.

Negligence: According to Layon (informally published data, USJA Coaching Symposium, 2003, 2004), writing as legal council for the United States Judo Association and Martens (1990), writing for the American Coaching Effectiveness Program, coaches (regardless of sport) have nine legal duties:

    i) Plan the activity
    ii) Provide proper instruction

iii)	Provide a safe training environment	
iv)	Provide and maintain adequate and appropriate training equipment	
v)	Match your players appropriately for size, age, ability or other factors that might be important	
vi)	Supervise your players	
vii)	Evaluate your players for injury	
viii)	Warn of risks	
ix)	Provide appropriate levels of emergency assistance	

If you fail in any of these duties then you could be found negligent and subject to civil action. In general, for a coach to be found negligent, it is normally necessary to demonstrate that the coach had a legal duty that was not performed, and which resulted in injury or loss to a player to whom the coach owed the duty (Martens, 1990). Although we have mentioned many of these issues in earlier sections, it is good to remind ourselves of them again in this section.

We have already mentioned planning the activity through the use of lesson plans and the development of a syllabus. This area of coach preparation will be examined in detail in Levels II & III. When considering negligence, the most obvious aspect of proper planning involves the introduction of advanced drills to students who have not been adequately prepared. Consequently, if you do not consider the physical and mental preparedness of your players when introducing a drill you may be negligent in your duty to adequately plan the activity. As an example, let us say that you have an overweight person who joins the dojo to lose weight and in the first week you have that person doing vigorous randori. Let us further say that this person is having a difficult time breathing and keeping up. There is a risk of negligence here, primarily because you as a coach should know better than to expect an overweight person to do vigorous randori when his or her body is not yet ready for such activities. In this example, providing a lower intensity drill for the player who is not ready for vigorous randori and reminding that person to live within his or her limits would be all that is required to remove the risk entirely.

A final part of proper preparation involves record keeping. Keep a file of written lesson plans. If a player gets injured on your mat and then comes back several weeks, months or years later to seek compensation for his or her injuries, will you be able to remember your lesson plan for the night of the injury? If there is an injury, keep a record of the event and clip a copy of your lesson plan to the report. You will then have two copies of the lesson plan: One in your master file, and one in the student's file.

You also have a duty to provide appropriate instruction, which means that you must teach according to accepted practices of Judo and you must teach using accepted practices for the age of your students. As an example, if you teach neck bridges as part of the class, or for any reason whatsoever, you are being negligent. There is extreme risk to the vertebrae in this sort of action. Simply put, it is not an accepted practice. On the other hand doing a shoulder bridge would be a much safer alternative and remove the risk to the neck. An example of not providing age appropriate instruction is teaching full force arm bars to a six year-old child. Children's bodies are still growing and applying joint locks can cause damage to young, under-developed bones. Moreover, children have different learning needs and different learning styles. If you have to have children and adults on the mat at the same time, provide different lesson plans for each group. As a final comment here, teaching according to accepted practices of Judo simply means using common sense, protecting your players while they practice, not exposing them to unnecessary risks and playing by the rules.

We should also touch on vicarious liability in this segment. If you have assistant coaches helping you teach, or even teaching for you when you are away, **you are still responsible for the results of the assistant's teaching**. Simply put, if you are the chief instructor you cannot delegate your legal duties. It is permissible to have assistants, but if they are working under your authority, you are legally bound for negligence as though you were teaching the students yourself.

The next duties that fall to the coach are related to each other and include the obligation to provide a safe training environment and to provide and maintain equipment. For the Judo coach, the mat is the most important piece of training equipment we use. You should make sure that the mat is firm and yet can cushion a fall. It should not be torn, or have holes in it. If it is covered, the cover should not be torn or have holes and/or wrinkles in it. There should be an adequate safety area for traffic around the mats. The surface upon which the mats are set is another consideration. Using thin ethafoam mats resting directly on a concrete floor could easily be seen as a negligent practice. The walls and floor of the dojo should be clear of objects such as nails, splinters, or objects that can become dislodged or fall.

Ensure that there is adequate lighting in all areas of the dojo including the restrooms and the changing areas. Keep chemicals out of reach of children.

If you do not own or rent the facility in which you train, get into the habit of doing a regular check of the physical spaces (training floor, dressing rooms, restrooms, travel areas) before class. Remove and/or warn of potential environmental hazards. Like it or not, cleanliness is another aspect of a safe training environment and says a lot to your students about what things you value. An instructor who takes time to make sure things are clean, cared for and safe, is much more likely to teach in a similar fashion, than one who does not.

The use of weapons is not a big part of Judo except for the practice of kata such as Goshin Jutsu and Kime No Kata. In instances where weapons are used, keep them stored away from students who do not know how to use them and make sure that the weapons are safe to use. When using wooden sticks and knives make sure that they are free of splinters. Never practice with a live blade.

The next area of concern is matching your players for size, age and/or ability and then discharging your obligation to supervise the activities of your students closely. It is your duty to ensure that your players are not matched in such a way as to place one in a significantly disadvantageous position relative to the other. To do so increases the risk of injury and is cause for accusations of negligence. Consequently you must consider not just size, age or ability but level of physical conditioning, attitude, maturity and experience. It is your responsibility to intervene if your students are mismatched or are not adhering to the expected levels of cooperation or control, which brings us to the duty of supervision.

Supervision requires that the coach be on the mat while training takes place. Equally, the coach should maintain a position from which he or she can observe the entire mat. Turning your back on a group of students to offer specific supervision to a smaller group of students can be considered negligent. Look at it from this perspective: you have several pairs working together performing a drill. You go over to one particular pair to offer advice and then an injury occurs behind you. When the insurance adjusters call and ask you what you saw, you are obliged to tell them that you didn't see the incident because your back was inadvertently turned when the event occurred. It now moves into the realm of possible negligence. Could you have prevented the event had you been paying attention? If the answer is yes, you have failed in your duty to supervise your players and can then be found negligent. Supervision on its own, however, is not enough. You must be willing to act swiftly to reduce risk or deal with an emergency.

The foregoing brings us to the next duties, which involve evaluating your players for their ability to participate and for any possible injury. As a coach, it is your responsibility to ensure that your players are healthy enough to take part in your classes.

You must watch for signs of fatigue or loss of concentration, since both are pre-incident indicators and both raise your risk factors dramatically. Always allow free access to water and rest. Likewise, when frustration sets in, consider breaking down the drill in order to preserve a safe training environment and to raise the level of comprehension.

Since Judo is such a close, personal activity, it is important to make sure that your players are not contagious in any way. If a student has a disability, health concern, or is recovering from an injury it is advisable to get a doctor's permission before returning to practice. When a student does return to training after an injury-induced lay-off, the coach should be cognizant that the psychological trauma may take longer to heal than the physiological injury. By way of illustration, students who suffer a knee injury may be reluctant to depend on the affected leg when they first return to class even if their doctor has told them that the knee is now fine. It is the psychological fear of re-injury that holds the student back. Placing fearful students in a situation they fear is an increased risk factor and requires wisdom and understanding on the part of the coach.

If there is an injury on or off the mat, it is the duty of the coach to provide emergency assistance. Unless you are a medical professional you are not licensed to provide medical treatment. You are however expected to provide emergency assistance (Martens, 1990; Flegel, 1992; Handal, 1992). Take a first-aid course and get CPR certification. Keep both current and encourage all of your upper ranks and assistant instructors to do the same. If an injury occurs, remove the student from the activity, find out from the student and witnesses what happened before you move, inspect or touch the injury. The next stage is to inspect the injury and ask questions about what the student feels. The last stage is to touch the injury and the limit of your assistance should be to "immobilize and transport." Flegel (1992) recommends the use of the H.I.T. rule, which means History, Inspect, and then

Touch. As soon as possible after the event, make a written report for the student's file.

You can treat minor cuts, scrapes, bruises and abrasions that are a natural part of Judo training. You should **not** treat any suspected joint, muscle, bone or head injury. When we talk about treatment, we are talking about resetting a broken bone or similar sorts of activities for which most coaches are not qualified.

> "Treatment, as such, implies that the provider is the primary care-giver and adequately suited and trained for complete management of [the] injury, to include recognition of complications which may ensue, that services may be remunerative, that judgment must be exercised for the necessity of further testing, referral to specialists, or tertiary care" (Gary Berliner M.D., Pers. Comm., 2001).

When we talk about being a provider of emergency assistance we are referring to your ability to check whether the injured person is breathing, has a pulse or is bleeding (American Red Cross, 1993; Handal, 1992). As an emergency provider your main role is to ensure that an injured person is stabilized and comfortable and to sustain the well-being of the injured player to the best of your ability, until qualified medical help can be obtained. Your best advice when the injury is beyond the realm of simple first aid is always to obtain medical assistance when needed or to advise the student to do so. The key here is to do no more and no less than you are **qualified** to do for the injured student. As an example, if a student breaks a bone in your class and cuts through a blood vessel, you are not qualified to reset the bone, but you are expected to do what you can to stop the bleeding and call the emergency medical services. If a student loses consciousness during a Judo class, for whatever reason, do not let him or her return to practice until he or she has seen a health professional (Martens, 1990).

Keep written records, including a health history on each of your students. How would you like to recruit an apparently healthy individual and then watch the student have a heart attack on your mat during light randori? Wouldn't you prefer to know that the student had a pre-existing heart condition and had obtained a doctor's permission to participate, rather than be unaware of it until the event transpires before your eyes? If you know ahead of time, then the pair of you can monitor what the student does and jointly develop a training program that is appropriate for the medical condition. Having developed a joint program, you will have warned your student of the risks, obtained written consent and given written freedom to stop training whenever the student felt the need to do so. You are both now mutually aware of the training expectations and the medical situation.

Your last duty is to provide an explanation of inherent risks and obtain an agreement to participate. It is your duty to warn of the risks inherent in the drills you teach. When you teach something new, warn of the risks and provide reminders. Simply put, this means doing things like reminding students to turn their head when throwing forward, to use appropriate force, not to crank on an arm bar and to tap out when it locks.

Use waivers and risk agreements (see Appendix) and be prepared to discuss them with your students. Have students sign a new waiver each year and for any special events. Keep written records, even the old waivers.

Summary: Like it or not, litigation is a fact of our society. Ignorance of your duties is no excuse and failure to ensure the safety of your players will lead you into legal hassles. To protect yourself:

i) Keep it professional
ii) Keep written records
iii) Remember always that your prime responsibility is the safety of your players.

V. Physical Principles

Many of the actions in a Judo class can be related to simple biomechanical principles and the basic physical laws, which govern the movement of bodies through space. The references cited give some account of some of these principles, but are not intended to be either inclusive or comprehensive (Campbell, 1974; Judo Canada, 1983; Leggett, 1978; Luttgens and Wells, 1989; Watanabe and Avakian, 1960; Weers, 1995, 1998, 2003).

Adversarial Psychology: This is not exactly a biomechanical principle so much as a psychological tool. Adversarial psychology essentially dictates that in an attacker-defender situation, an attacker will want whatever the defender does not want. Adversarial psychology therefore has a lot to say about how to deal with an opponent who is attempting to develop a power grip or who is exerting some force against your body. If, for example, an opponent grabs your jacket, he or she expects that you will pull away. If you pull away, then the opponent will want the exact opposite, so he or she grips more tightly and tugs against your pull. The logical action is to respond when your opponent tugs at the jacket by adding your force to your opponent's in the direction of the pull. It is then easy to capitalize on your opponent's grip and turn it to your advantage. The physical principle, which emerges from this, is the principle of realignment and redirection of force.

In most randori settings, the exchange often looks more like a tug of war between opposing forces, than a flow and counter flow of energy between two bodies. Resisting a push will only create an antagonistic tug of war, which the stronger player will win. By way of contrast, blending with the oncoming force and redirecting it will cause attackers to over-extend and off-balance themselves, because the expected reaction force never materialized. Judo Kata (and perhaps most especially Ju No Kata) teach us this very same principle over and over, which is perhaps why Leggett (1978) was such a proponent of learning kata. Instead of meeting a push head on and creating a reaction force against it, skilled Judoka will realign themselves with the force and redirect it to their own advantage.

Sun Tzu (Ames, 1993) states that we are most vulnerable when we consider ourselves to be invincible. Whenever an attacker commits fully to a technique be it a throw, hold or strike, adversarial psychology dictates that there is an expectation of resistance. When the resistance (reaction force) does not materialize, the attacker is frequently left in a vulnerable position. By combining the mental concept of adversarial psychology with the biomechanical principle of realigning and redirecting force, a skilled Judoka can make the most efficient use both offensive and defensive actions.

Attack Space: The attack space is the distance between two players. According to Sun Tzu (Ames, 1993), whoever enters the attack space first, loses. An example of this principle at work is found when a student steps backward into a forward throw without first causing his or her partner to fall into the attack space by virtue of a superior off-balance. If the partner is falling into the attack space because the thrower's **movement** created an off-balance and **then** the attacker back steps under the person being thrown, the technique will be successful. If the thrower back steps without adequate preparation (person being thrown is still balanced), the attack is sure to be countered thus fulfilling another of Sun Tzu's statements: "Invincibility lies in defense, the possibility of victory lies in the attack." The student who understands the attack space and how to control it, also knows:

    i)   What strategic actions will be effective for any given attack space.

    ii)   Which of the opponent's attacks need to be blocked and/or countered and which ones do not represent a threat.

    iii)   What attacks and counterattacks can be launched effectively and

    iv)   How to lure the other player into the attack space in order to create vulnerability.

Balance: The irreducible essence of Judo is concerned with an understanding and appreciation of posture and position. Remember that without good posture and position it is difficult to execute an effective offense or defense, therefore "Position is King". Weers (2203), makes a very valid point that we tend to forget to teach posture as a fundamental skill in Judo; that is we forget it until we see bad posture and then we act to correct it. It would be better to emphasize the elements of good posture as an acquirable skill set from the onset of training. Do not forget however, that posture is not just the spatial arrangement of the human structure. Posture is also an attitude of mind and condition of spirit (Herrigel, 1953; Leggett, 1978; Morgan, 1992; Nakamura, 1992), which is often revealed in the physical posture. For the sake of this discussion, however, we shall confine our thoughts to the physical aspects of balance. There are three aspects of balance:

i) Visual, based upon what our eyes tell us concerning our position in space.
ii) Vestibular, based upon the response of the inner ear to gravity and motion.
iii) Proprioceptive, based upon a muscular awareness of pressure changes in our joints.

We obtain a visual awareness of our position in space through the use of environmental cues that provide information concerning our orientation relative to the environment in which we are moving. Secondly, vestibular balance awareness is provided by the inner ear, which collects static and dynamic equilibrium information. Static equilibrium is obtained through an awareness of the body's position with respect to gravity, whereas dynamic equilibrium relates to maintaining posture in the face of changes in body velocity and or body rotations. Thirdly, small-scale muscular and joint adjustments provide proprioceptive information concerning balance as we move. Proprioceptive movements are neuromuscular reflex actions that finely tune the body as it moves. Proprioceptive awareness provides information concerning changes in muscle tension and changes in the position of a joint. It is the proprioceptive aspect of balance that is so critical to the martial artist. It is possible to train proprioceptive awareness using one-leg balance drills, or ball-balancing drills. It is also possible to take away our tendency to rely upon visual cues by working with eyes closed and "feeling" the position and balance of our opponents (Luttgens and Wells, 1989).

The maintenance of positional stability in the dynamic environment of the Judo mat is the result of developing and practicing good balance and good posture. Being aware of the position of your center of gravity and keeping it within the base of support through the use of good posture is essential to developing good balance. Good balance can be defined as (Leggett, 1978; Weers, 1995, 2003):

i) Keeping your weight evenly distributed.
ii) Weight over the balls of the feet.
iii) Head up and centered over the shoulders.
iv) Hips unlocked.
v) Center forward.
vi) Center of gravity directly at, or below, the center of balance and centered over the base of support.
vii) *Keep your nose between your toes*

Balance Lines: A balance line is an imaginary line that joins the balls of the feet. The easiest off-balances are produced by creating force perpendicular to a balance line. Any static stance is a target for the application of force. Consequently, if a Judoka is frequently changing stances in a dynamic setting, he or she will be less vulnerable to attack, especially if the stances are accompanied by good posture.

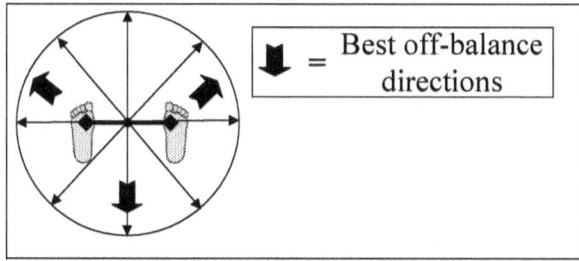

Figure 9: Classical Happo No Kuzushi, the Eight Directions of off-balance in Judo

The classical Happo No Kuzushi (Figure 9) demonstrates the forms of off-balance (Kano, 1986). According to the theory, in a normal, upright stance with the feet about shoulder wide and center faced forward, there are eight directions in which it is possible to off-balance the body: the four corners, front, back and to the sides. The off-balance to the rear is easier to create than forward off-balance to the front simply as a function of our anatomical arrangement having toes pointing forwards. Another excellent off balance is to draw a player out over the little toe side of the foot, where again, there is no base of support for the upper body. **The key to any off balancing act is to separate the player's upper body weight from his or her support structure and in so doing, create an unstable body arrangement.** This sort of arrangement can be created by either: a) holding the upper body in place and taking out the support from below, or b) holding the support structure in place and pushing the upper body beyond its support.

There are several principles of balance (modified from Luttgens and Wells, 1989) with which students of Judo will become personally acquainted as they journey through the learning process.

    i. Positional stability is greatest when the center of gravity is directly over the mid point of a line drawn between the balls of the feet.
    ii. Stability decreases as the center of gravity moves towards the outside edge of the foot (little toe side).
    iii. Stability decreases as the center of gravity moves towards the heels of the feet.
    iv. The lower the center of gravity, the greater the stability of the body.

v. The wider the base of support, the lower the potential for mobility.
vi. The greater the mass, the greater the stability, or resting inertia.

Biomechanics and the Summation of Forces: The human body is a collection of plates and rods and the connectors that enable the plates and rods to move relative to each other. From the perspective of movement, the human body consists of articulating joints composed of bones, which provide the structural framework; muscles and tendons, which work the joints; and ligaments that hold the joints together. Biomechanically, the joints of the human body can be used to create only three types of action:

i. Pushing
ii. Pulling
iii. Twisting

In order to effect these actions, the joints must be required complete sequential activities in a specific order. For instance: In order to push effectively with a hand and arm, you must unlock and rotate the shoulder girdle, unfold the arm at the elbow and rotate the wrist. As a direct consequence of their construction the human joints are capable of only certain types of motion that confer a range of motion for each joint according to its particular construction. For instance the knee joint is primarily a hinge joint, which can open and close, whereas the hip joint is a ball and socket joint, which can complete a wider range of motions. It is therefore possible to define types of joint action as follows:

i. Flexion and Extension. Flexion decreases the angle at the joint (e.g. bringing the fingertips towards shoulder by bending the elbow), whereas extension increases the angle at the joint (e.g. moving the fingertips away from the shoulder by straightening the arm through the elbow joint).

ii. Abduction and Adduction. Abduction moves a limb away from the body, whereas adduction brings the limb closer to the body (e.g. abduction at the shoulder joint and girdle moves the arm away from the side and adduction brings the arm towards the side).

iii. Rotation. Rotation of a joint involves a turning or twisting motion of one surface of the joint relative to the other (e.g. twisting the spine or turning the wrist over).

The point to all of this, is that in order to understand how a throw can be achieved most effectively it is necessary to recognize that during the action, each joint required to complete the skill, will be needed to generate part of the necessary force at a particular time in the process. The example that we used earlier (pushing with the arm or hand) is a relatively simple action, but Judo throws are very complex, full body actions that involve many joints working together to create the force required to complete the throw. During a throwing action, the student's joints may be required to do at least three things: Support the student's weight, support his or her partner's weight and provide part of the force that projects his or her partner through the air and onto the planet. It is important therefore, that each joint be used in the correct sequence to deliver the maximum power output at the moment of throw. Summation of forces requires that joints be used in order from large joints to small joints during the execution of the technique. Consequently, if your players can create an approximation of a required skill using large body actions, it will then be possible to refine the skill by paying attention to both the specific types of joint actions and the timing of the actions. It is for this reason that we encourage you to teach gross biomechanical actions first and worry about the details later. After all, what does it matter if your player has his or her little finger in exactly the right place if the hip block is completely out of alignment?

Body Turning and Rotation: When an effective throw is executed, it is necessary for Tori to twist the hips and turn the head in the direction of the throw. In order to make effective throws it is therefore necessary to employ both vertical body rotations and horizontal body rotations. Vertical rotations involve actions such as bending at the knees, or bending forward at the waist, whereas horizontal rotations include actions such as hip and shoulder rotations.

When we execute a forward throwing action such as O Goshi or Seoi Nage it will be necessary to rotate your opponent's shoulders and back to the mat. When throwing the opponent to the rear in such actions as O Soto Gari it will be necessary for you to push them onto their back and for you to bend forward at the waist. In sacrifice techniques like Tomoe Nage you will need to bend your partner at the waist as you project your opponent's body over your head using your foot as a fulcrum causing your opponent to be rotated onto his or her back.

"Center": Many martial arts talk about the center and how to control it. In this section we are only concerned with the biophysical aspects of being centered. Being biomechanically centered involves keeping your hands in front of your shoulders and your shoulders in front of your hips. Also make sure that your elbows are kept down and in towards your sides (Weers, 2003).

If the hands are not centered, then they are in a weak position relative to the application of the power needed for the throw. If the hands are in front of the shoulders and the shoulders in front of the hips, then the body rotations will produce maximum efficiency in the throw (all other factors being equal).

Driving Leg: All Judo actions, whether they are hold-downs and throws or whether they are aspects of movement and gripping, derive their power from pushing against something stable. The most stable thing against which we can push is the planet, so the driving leg pushes into the planet, which creates a reaction force with which we can create an action. This is in conformity with Newton's third law of motion, which states that to every action there is an equal, and opposite action.

Figure 10: A randori session showing O Uchi Gari attack with a driver placed opposite the hole. Tori's driving leg is pushing towards the hole and Tori's right hand is pushing to Uke's lower left side. Given the lack of body contact between the two players, had Uke's right foot been placed more advantageously he would have been able to rotate his body and counter the technique, but as events transpired the attack ended in Tori's favor with a Kesa-style hold-down on Uke's left side.

In order for a technique to be successful, it is necessary for the driving leg to be placed opposite the destination point of the technique (Campbell, 1974), that is to say be parallel to the direction of application of the force (push). This brings up a rather neat point: All throws and ground holds are necessarily **pushing actions** (Weers, 1995, 2003). From the perspective of basic physics, if you consider that the driving leg of any throw is pushing into the planet, then it becomes clear that the reaction force will be used to push the person being thrown into the planet.

Figure11: Kesa Gatame with the attacker's left foot well placed to drive his weight to his opponent's opposite shoulder.

The Hole: All throws and hold-downs are predicated upon the existence of a "hole." If you think of a human being as not having enough legs, then the idea of a hole is easier to understand. Basically if you are off-balanced, you must move a foot or lean against something in order to re-establish equilibrium. In fact, by way of illustration, the whole process of walking is about deliberately losing and regaining balance just before we fall over.

Since we do in fact only have two legs, any time that our center of gravity falls outside of the base of support we experience a positive response to gravity, unless the base of support can be established below the center of gravity. The sensation of being off-balanced is one of a void opening up in the direction of the off-balance. In Judo, we call this "the hole." Whenever an opponent is being thrown, there is only one place into which he or she can be effectively thrown with the minimum application of force. This means that the hole is directly in front of the direction of off-balance and that the attacker's driving leg must be placed directly opposite the hole, so that the push will be directly into the hole. Any other configuration of the two bodies will result in an ineffective throw.

Relative to your partner's position, there are only three possible positions for the opponent's support foot. Knowledge of these positions will indicate the location of the hole into which the opponent must fall (Weers 1995, 2003):

> i) If the opponent's support foot is to the rear, on the side away from the attacker then the main hole will be to the far side front corner (Hidden Foot or Forward Hole),

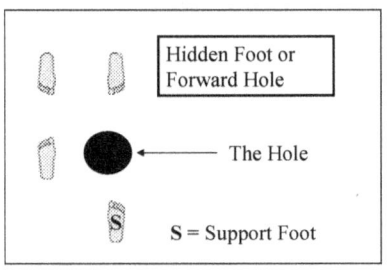

Figure 12: The Hidden Foot.

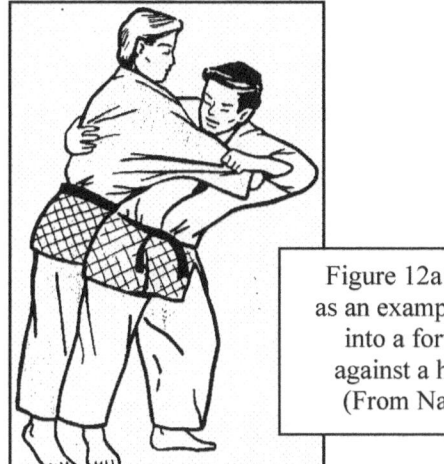

Figure 12a: Uki Goshi, as an example of a throw into a forward hole, against a hidden foot. (From Nauta, 1996)

Figure 12b: Seoi Nage used as a throw into a forward hole

ii) If the support foot is forward on the side away from the attacker, then the main hole will be to the far side rear corner (Exposed or Advanced Foot or Rear Hole),

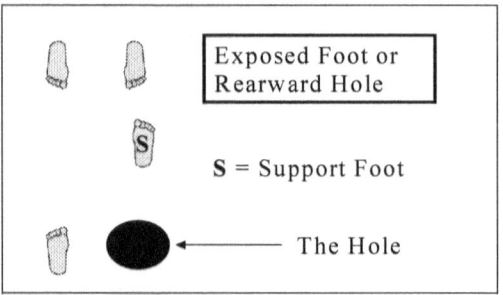

Figure13 The Exposed Foot.

Figure 13a: Ko Uchi Maki Komi, as an example of a throw into a rear hole against a forward support foot. (From Nauta, 1996)

Figure13b: Ko Uchi Maki Komi attacking into a rear hole

iii) If the support foot is between the two players, then the main hole will be to the close side, rear corner (Trespassing Foot or Intervening Hole).

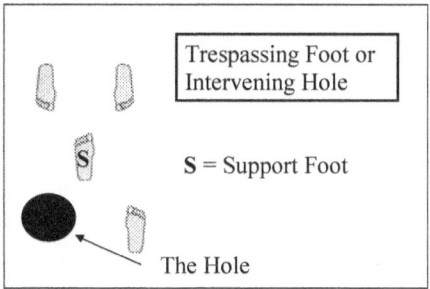

Figure 14: The Trespassing Foot.

Figure 14a: Ko Soto Gari, as an example of a throw into an intervening hole, against a trespassing foot. (From Nauta, 1996)

Figure 14b: Tani Otoshi used as an attack against a trespassing foot

Given these three basic positions of the defender's support foot relative to the attacker, it becomes clear that the hole is where the support foot is not and also not where the attacker is standing since he or she is blocking a potential hole.

In a situation where the weight is evenly balanced, the student is in what can be called a square mobile posture and must therefore be induced to step before a hole can be established (Figure 15). In the square mobile posture the weight is equally balanced and your opponent can choose to move to either side to protect himself or herself. Sun Tzu (Ames, 1993) puts it rather neatly "Know where your opponent is strong and avoid him there."

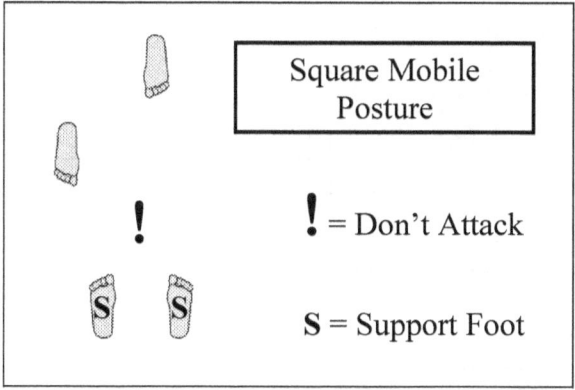

Figure 15: Square Mobile Posture

The Hop Reflex: In Judo, there are times when it is possible to create a reflex action in your partner's supporting foot that creates an opportunity to throw. In effect, your partners will throw themselves. If you draw someone forward to an off-balance position over his or her lead foot, there will come a point when your partner is standing on one leg and the heel of the support (lead) foot will come up. At this moment all the weight will be centered over the ball of the foot and the knee on the support leg will lock. If you extend the off-balance just a little further your partner will "hop" to regain balance. This is also called the "metatarsal stretch reflex." The application of the reflex is that if you apply a throwing technique (such as Uki Otoshi or Hiza Guruma) to the support leg at the exact moment that your opponent hops, then your opponent will be completely dependent upon your body for positional stability (Figures 16, 16a).

Figure 16: Uki Otoshi as an example of a throw utilizing the hop reflex. (From Nauta, 1996)

Figure 16a: Uki Otoshi caught in the moment of the "hop"

Levers: Knowledge of levers is also important to the student of Judo, since levers provide a mechanical advantage when applying force to a resistance. Most players use levers at an intuitive level and could not tell you that a specific skill requires a specific type of lever in order to be effective. Indeed an intimate knowledge of levers by your players will not necessarily improve their performance. Conversely, the ineffective execution of a skill can sometimes be related to the ineffective placement or use of a lever. Consequently, the coach who can see that it is the lever that needs to be adjusted, will be able to coach his or her players more effectively. There are three classes of levers that are used in throwing and joint locking (Figure 17).

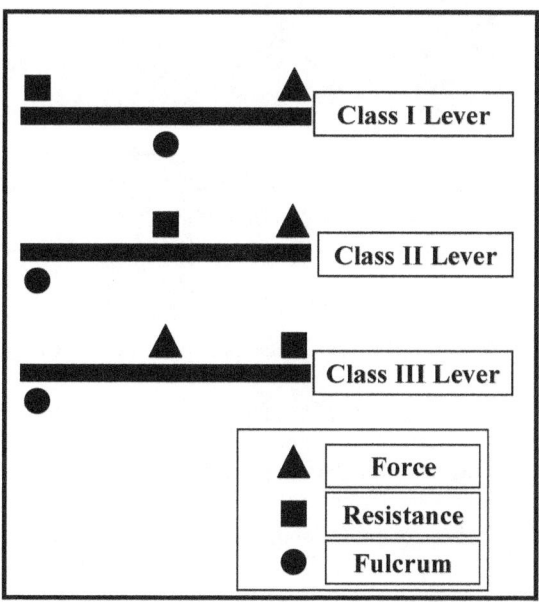

Figure 17: The Classes of Levers

Class one levers have the fulcrum placed somewhere between the force being applied and the resistance to the force. The greater the distance between the applied force and the fulcrum, the more effective is the lever. Some elbow locking techniques are class one levers (Figure 18).

Figure 18: Waki Gatame used as an example of a class one lever.

Class two levers place the resistance between the fulcrum and the force being applied. Once again, the closer the resistance is to the fulcrum the more effective is the lever. Foot propping techniques such as Tai Otoshi (Figure 19) and Uki Otoshi are examples of class two levers (Watanabe and Avakian, 1960).

Figure 19: Tai Otoshi used as an example of a class two lever.

Class three levers place the force being applied between the fulcrum and the resistance. In this case the force being applied needs to be closer to the resistance to maximize efficiency of the lever. Several elbow-locking techniques are class three levers (Figure 20).

Figure 20: Ude Gatame used as an example of a class three lever during an open randori session

Moving Off-line: It is an axiom that the best way to avoid a trap is to not be there when it is sprung. The same principle is evident throughout martial arts training. In the movie "Dune", the Mentat Thufir Howat, tells young Prince Paul Atreides that the first step in avoiding a trap is knowing of its existence. This advice implies that you have an awareness of your opponent's actions.

A clear understanding of body movement will supply pre-incident indicators of an impending attack. There are only so many ways in which a human body can move and given one starting position, it is possible to predict with reasonable accuracy, what will happen next as a consequence of any movement emerging from the original position.

Learning to avoid an attack by moving off-line and being able to redirect the opponent's energy is one of the key performance goals of the skilled Judoka. Moving off-line requires that we not resist our opponent's attacks, but rather flow with them and use them to our advantage. Weers (2003), provides an elegant discussion of the development of countering skills. In his discussion, Weers (2003) compares timing and outcome as it relates to the effective use of countering skills. Ultimately the best use of countering skills is when there is "nobody home" when the initial attacker commits fully to his or her attack. In this scenario, the defender sees the impending attack as it develops and is able to place his or her body in a position that maximizes any opportunity that exists for exploiting the initial attacker's actions. Probably one of the best tournament examples of this principle is the effective use of Sukashi actions against a fully committed Uchi Mata attack.

The tricky part to all of this is to keep our opponent thinking that we are unaware of his or her strategy until he or she has fully committed to a course of action and cannot alter the plan of attack.

Plyometric Action: Many forceful bursts of activity in Judo are plyometric in nature. A plyometric action uses the elastic properties of a muscle to assist in a forceful contraction. You may recall from the section on stretching that two sets of muscles are used for flexing and extending any joint. These two-muscle sets work in such a way that the contracting muscle (known as the agonist) creates the joint movement and the antagonist muscle on the opposite side of the joint relaxes and stretches (Luttgens and Wells, 1989). During plyometric action the agonist muscle is contracted so much that the antagonistic muscle on the opposite side of the joint is stretched to its elastic limit. When the agonist is relaxed, the elastic stretch reflex causes the antagonist muscles to start contracting, allowing for a more rapid and forceful generation of power. The elastic stretch reflex occurs because once a muscle is fully stretched it automatically contracts; this is also known as the "myotactic stretch reflex."

A good example of this principle at work involves the sudden, powerful burst of muscular effort used in a throw during which the competitor coils like a spring immediately prior to pushing into the throw. Two good examples in Judo are the drive out of a deep squat into a Seoi Nage type action or the application of Ura Nage in Nage no Kata. We will discuss plyometric power in more detail in the Level II manual.

Power Curve: Every technique has a power curve, which is related to energy generated and distance traveled over time. In the simplest example, a throw can only produce a finite amount of power during its execution. As the throw travels towards the planet it picks up momentum and obeys the equation:

$$F = M \times A.$$

Where:

F = Force upon impact

M = Mass of the body

A = Acceleration (rate of increase in distance traveled per unit time)

There comes a point however, on the journey that the throw has reached its maximum velocity and since the projected mass has not changed, the force produced has peaked. During any throwing action, the explosive development of the throw reaches a peak after which the energy is dissipated and the throw loses power. Once the thrower's power has peaked however, a well-executed throw will derive additional force from the acceleration due to gravity. This is why powerful tournament throws continue to pick up momentum as the thrower's energy is replaced by the acceleration due to gravity.

Conversely, any travel away from the planet after the attacker's power spike is reached will only cause the dissipation of energy and the loss of power, (Figure 21). A good example of this sort of thing comes from the ineffective application of O Soto Gari, where the attacker has not developed a good angle of attack into the appropriate hole and the defender is forced merely to step backwards but is not seriously threatened.

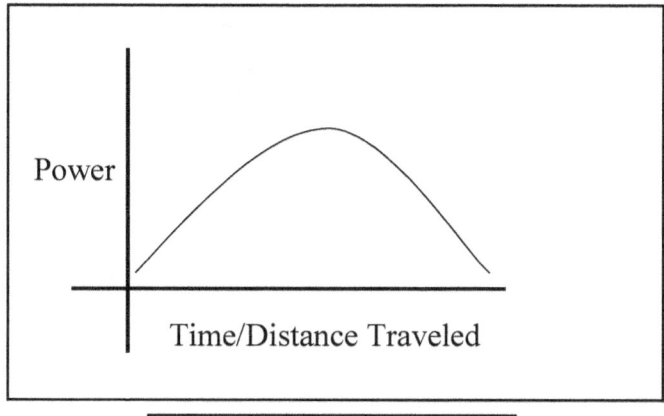

Figure 21: The Power Curve.

A simple rule that can be applied to the power curve is that maximum power is achieved in the last few inches of a technique. This is especially true in regard to throwing techniques, which only reach their maximum potential power with a full rotation of the body.

The Power Arm (Side): The power arm or side is the arm or the side of the body that transmits the force of the attack into the opponent's body (Campbell, 1974; Weers, 1995, 2003). In Judo, power is necessarily transmitted by pushing into the opponent. The driving leg is aligned with the power arm and both are being employed in the same direction with an optimal angle of attack towards the hole into which we shall deposit our opponent. It is important to recognize that it is **not** just the power hand that drives into the opponent during a committed attack (Campbell, 1974), but includes the **entire arm and the side of the body** (Weers,

1995, 2003). It is equally important to remember that throwing power comes out of the hips, not out of the hands and shoulders. The driving leg provides a pushing force into the planet; the reaction force from the planet is then transferred **through the hips** to the body parts that will make the action. The power of any technique is therefore effectively transmitted through the use of a complete hip rotation.

In most cases the maximum amount of force is delivered when two bodies are moving towards each other. It is therefore advisable to have your opponent moving **toward** your power arm. One of the simplest examples of this type of action is when the defender steps toward the attacker's power arm and gets his or her leg sliced out with an O Uchi Gari type of action just as the defender commits weight to the stepping leg.

A corollary to the statement in the previous paragraph is that it is very difficult to push effectively against something that is moving away from you, unless you are moving faster than your opponent. Throwing actions, however, can and do happen under these circumstances in situations where the defender is retreating backwards and the attacker is bringing the force of the attack to bear upon the defender at a faster rate than he or she can retreat. An example here would be when the attack is a driving O Soto Gari and the defender commits weight to the leg being attacked as he or she retreats.

On the other side of the body, away from the power arm, is the **locking hand**. The purpose of the locking hand is to hold your opponent in place while you execute your technique. Consequently, the locking hand traps the opponent close to you and restricts the effective use of defensive maneuvers such as turnouts.

As a final comment concerning the position of the power hand, the placement of the power hand will vary according to the force required to execute a skill. In general foot sweeps, which require a low level of pushing force can be executed with a high grip, whereas throws that require a high level of force such as Ura Nage will require that the power hand is placed much closer to the defender's hips.

Realignment and Redirection of Force: In a battle in which forces collide, the larger force will always emerge the victor. In Judo, the essential truth is to use your opponent's force against him or her by adding it to your own force pushing in a particular direction (Kano, 1986). We have already discussed the application of realignment and redirection of force, several times in this section. As an instructor, one of your performance goals should be to bring your students to an appreciation that fighting strength for strength is a futile exercise.

Support Foot: By definition, the support foot is the foot that bears your weight. It can also be referred to as the weighted leg. Understanding the principle of the support foot or weighted leg is essential to making the human structure collapse. As a rule throwing actions should attack the support foot. The best time to attack is when the opponent's weight has been fully committed to the impending step. In the moment in which a defender has chosen to fully commit to a step he or she is vulnerable to attack. If the defender has no weight on the foot being attacked, it is easy to move the leg out of the way of the attack and to create a counter attack.

Any time you have more force available for use in a particular situation, than your opponent, you have a tactical advantage. The essence of the matter is that once your opponent has committed to a course of action (making a step), the foot on which the weight is placed becomes a target for attack. We should also be aware that in addition to the weighted foot, other are variables involved in movement, such as whether a player is moving towards or away from the attacker or whether a player is leaning towards or away from the attacker.

Conversely, the leg that bears no weight is the free leg and can be used to attack or defend, sweep, hook or trap the opponent's leg (Weers, 1995). The free leg can be a target for attack in order to cause an opponent to stumble and/or encourage them to commit weight from one leg to the other; but if a throw is to be successful, the throwing action must take the support out from under the opponent's body.

There is also a warning here: Your opponent's support foot in Judo is also his or her driving leg and is therefore the support upon which the rest of the weaponry is arranged. Placing yourself between the opponent's support foot and your own off-balance hole would not be wise.

Timing: Learning to time the tactical use (application) of a skill is a lesson in precision. If the skill is the least bit too early or too late, the effectiveness will not be as great. A well-timed skill will therefore reach its power peak at the moment of greatest vulnerability of the opponent.

Timing evolves from a thorough understanding of force lines, speed, direction, distance and range, combined with a knowledge of the possible outcomes of any given action by an opponent. Since there are a limited number of movement possibilities from any given originating position, it follows that the Judoka, who can accurately predict the next move, will also have the edge for timing his or her next attack or defense.

With a clear understanding of the pre-incident indicators, it is possible for skilled Judoka to arrive in a position and simply wait for opponents to arrive at the moment of execution.

There is a relationship between the attacker and the opponent, which affects timing. The relationship is based upon the preparedness of the attacker and the vulnerability of the defender as follows:

    i)   When your opponent is about to attack, he or she concentrating so hard on his or her own technique that blindness often exists for the need for personal defense. (Sun Tzu...you are most vulnerable when you think you are invincible).

    ii)   When a player attacks and then withdraws he or she is extremely vulnerable to counter attack.

    iii)   When your opponent is blocking your first attack, he or she is vulnerable to combination techniques, because the defensive tools are already pre-occupied. Invariably, defensive tactics applied in one direction leave a player vulnerable to the application of a technique in exactly the opposite direction. The classic example here is the novice in randori who is induced block a hip throw only to be set up for a rear foot sweep.

    iv)   When your opponent pushes in the same direction as your technique, he or she cannot offer any resistance to your attack.

    v)   When the opponent has just finished breathing out, energy is at its lowest ebb. Breathing in is normally associated with increasing power and breathing out with dissipating power, therefore the best time to attack is at the end of an exhale, when your opponent has dissipated all his or her energy.

vi) When your opponent changes stances, direction or is off-balance.
vii) When your opponent has committed to a stepping action.
viii) When your opponent loses concentration.

A Final Comment: When executing a technique of any kind, there are several steps that will lead to a successful outcome as follows (modified from Weers, 1995, 2003):

i) Make sure your opponent is moving toward your power arm,
ii) Locate the support leg, and potential weapons,
iii) Decide upon a tactical solution (what skill to employ),
iv) Locate the hole into which you will push,
v) Assess your opponent's posture,
vi) Align your driver to be opposite the hole, center your weapons, adjust the angle of attack and execute,
vii) Expose your opponent's back to the mat, move your chest towards the hole.

In the final analysis, there are seven habits of highly effective judoka (Weers, 2003) that employ the physical principles we have discussed in this section and can be effectively taught using the conditions of learning we discussed earlier in the manual:

i) **Inside Power Hand**: The dominant player has his or her power hand placed inside the span of the shoulders, which allows the maximum application of force.

ii) **Feet Never Still**: The dominant player is never static when he or she is within gripping range of his or her partner.

iii) **Chest to the Hole**: If you are always driving your chest towards the mat, you are not exposing your back to the mat. By driving the chest towards the hole, the dominant player will maximize the commitment to the throwing or pinning opportunity and minimize the possibility of being scored upon.

iv) **Inside Leg Step Around**: By using an inside leg step around, an effective player will be placing his or her foot into the hole that the opponent had intended to exploit (Figure 22).

Figure 22: During a weak hip throw attempt, the defender uses the attack space to employ an inside leg step around to block the attack. In this instance the defender's grip is too high, her elbow and shoulder are compromised and she is therefore unable to take full advantage of her opportunity to counter attack.

v) **Uphill Turn**: Turning towards your opponent in a ground play situation reduces the exposure to the mat and creates the opportunity to increase the space between the attacker and your own body (Figure 23).

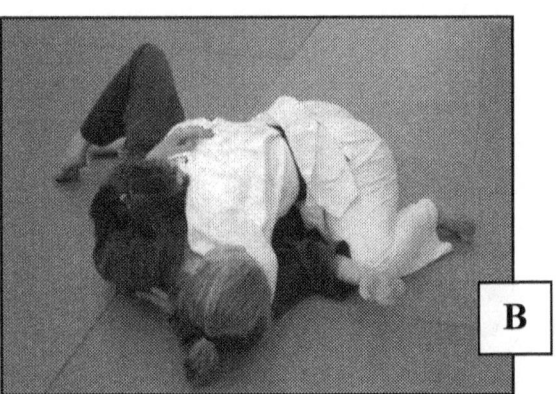

Figure 23: By using an uphill turn escape the defender is able to create space and reverse the pin.

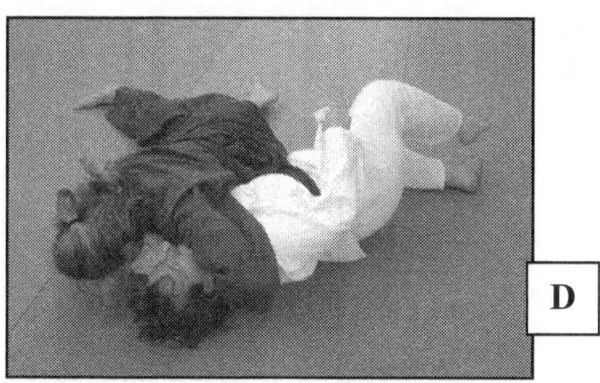

vi) **Knees off of the Mat**: By keeping knees off of the mat, an effective player does two things: Increases his or her mobility and increases the percentage of body mass that is resting on his or her opponent (Figure 24). Pat Burris, Olympic Coach is very fond of telling players to make their opponents bear their weight at all times. There are many sound reasons for this, not the least of which are the psychological pressure of feeling trapped and the greater level of energy that must be expended by a player who is carrying two person's weight.

Figure 24: In both these instances, the attackers are keeping knees off of the mat and placing weight on their opponents. Moreover, the defenders are being denied mobility while the attackers are free to move at will.

vii) **Position of Control**: A position of control exists any time you have the ability to move and your opponent does not. Equally, by applying the force at nearly a right angle to the opponent's chest an effective player maximizes the application of force. Conversely if a player wishes to improve his or her mobility it is necessary to "break the T".

VI. Tournaments

Although not an absolute requirement of practicing Judo, tournament participation is an integral part of the learning process for many Judo players. Often players enter the tournament arena without a clear understanding of how the tournament will be run so in this section we will be giving some guidance about how tournament divisions will be fought at most local and regional level events.

Tournament Divisions: In order to meet the sanctioning requirements of a Judo tournament; players are organized into fighting divisions according to gender, age and weight. If there are enough players, divisions may also be organized by rank into novice and "black belt" pools. At the local and regional level, most tournament directors fight the pools using one of two main methods:

- Double Elimination, in which players must normally lose twice before they are eliminated.
- Round Robin, in which everyone plays everyone else in the pool.

By understanding the tournament process and helping to guide your players through it, you will be able to allow your players to focus more fully on their matches and suggest appropriate tournament strategies. To that end we are going to discuss both the Round Robin and Double Elimination pool systems in some detail. We will use a typical eight man pool sheet for a modified double elimination division (Figure 25), work through an example for you (Figure 26) and give you a blank pool sheet, that you can adapt for your own needs (Appendix 6). We will also walk you through a four man round robin pool (Figures 27 & 28) and provide a blank round robin pool sheet in Appendix 7.

a. Double Elimination: In a double elimination division each player is guaranteed a minimum of two matches. Double elimination divisions can be contested in two ways. In one scenario the first place winner never loses a match and the best that the winner of the loser's bracket can do is take second place. Alternatively, it is possible for the winner of the loser's bracket to be given the opportunity to fight the winner of the winner's bracket to decide first and second places. In the example that we are using (Figures 25, 26) the player who does not lose is guaranteed first place and the winner of the loser's bracket will take second place. As a coach, it will be important for you to find out how the double elimination pools will be fought at each tournament that you attend with your players.

Double elimination divisions can be fought with any number of players, but if the number of contestants entered in a division is not a multiple of four or eight, then there will be byes. For instance, if your player is entered into a five person double elimination pool, there will be three byes in the first round (5 + 3 = 8), but if there are six in the division, then there will only be two byes (6 + 2 = 8). A bye automatically advances a player to the next round. The first time a player loses a match; he or she will enter the loser's pool. After the second loss your player will be eliminated. The sequence of events for an pool with eight players (Figure 25), shows that a player who loses in the first round will have to fight all the way through the loser's bracket in order to get a shot at second place.

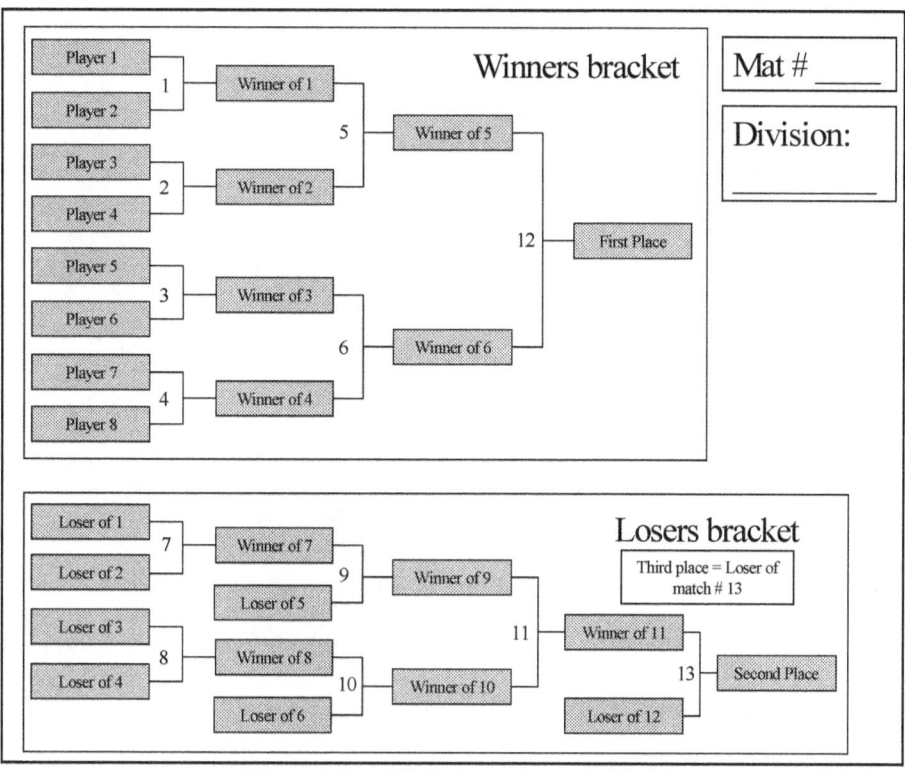

Figure 25: The flow of events for an eight-player "modified" double elimination division.

In our example (Figure 26) there are two byes in the first round because there were only six competitors entered. Consequently there are also two byes in the first round of the loser's bracket, because there will be two first round players who will not advance in the winners bracket. If you examine our example (Figure 26), Fred Watkins has a great day and wins every match to place first overall in the division. Chris Burton is the last person to lose in the winner's bracket and therefore in his next match he fights Joe Green, who has had to fight his way up the losers bracket.

Chris Burton wins the last match of the loser's bracket to take second place and Joe therefore takes third. Our example is therefore a "modified" double elimination tournament. It is at this point that the tournament director's choice comes into play. In our example, the winner of the last match in the loser's bracket (Chris Burton) has only lost one match, so technically he has not been eliminated. Consequently it is possible that Chris could be given the opportunity to fight Fred Watkins for first place. Some tournament directors take a strict view of first place and apply the logic that in order to place first you must not lose any matches (our example). In our example, Chris has already had a shot at the first place and lost, however, had Joe Green won the last match of the loser's bracket, then he never got a chance to fight Fred Watkins. Consequently, other tournament directors take a strict view of the double elimination component and have the winner of the loser's bracket fight the winner of the winner's bracket (conceivably twice) to determine a "true winner".

It is important for your players to know what type of double elimination tournament is being fought on the day. Normally this is announced in the tournament flier, but it is always a good idea to check with the pooling table and/or the tournament director on the day.

In the example that we have given you, Fred Watkins, Chris Burton, Joe Green, Bob Jones and Mike Reese all get more than two matches. John Smith however, is eliminated after his second match. You will also notice in our example that Joe Green has to fight Mike Reese twice; once in the winner's bracket and then once again in the loser's bracket. This can sometimes be confusing to both coaches and players, but is not unusual in double elimination tournaments. As a coach, it is a good idea to make a copy of the pool sheet, so that you can keep track of your player's progress. Understanding how the pool works saves time and aggravation for everyone concerned. As a reference tool after the tournament, the pool sheet used in conjunction with a video can be a very valuable learning tool.

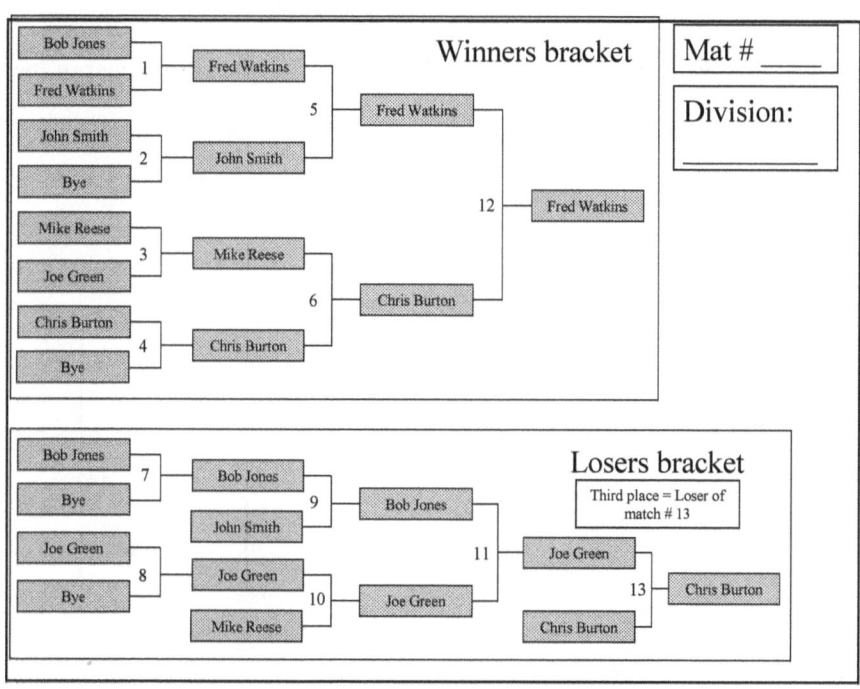

Figure 26: A six-player division contested at a double elimination tournament.

b. Round Robin: In a round robin division, everyone is matched against everyone else in the pool (Figure 27). Again, there are two ways to contest a round robin pool. Some tournament directors will award one point for a win, regardless of the "quality" of the win. In this scenario a win by koka gets the same value as a win by ippon. Other tournament directors feel that this encourages defensive play and therefore award points based upon the "quality" of the win. The actual number of points given for each type of win can vary from tournament to tournament, but the outcome is that in a point valued round robin division, it is not the number of wins that determines placement of medal winners, but the total number of points awarded to each player. This can be a source of confusion for players and coaches, especially if one player wins all his or her matches and does not take first place. If two players end up with the same aggregate score at the end of the day, then the winner of the match between the two players is given the higher standing. Alternatively, a run off match could be used to decide the final placement.

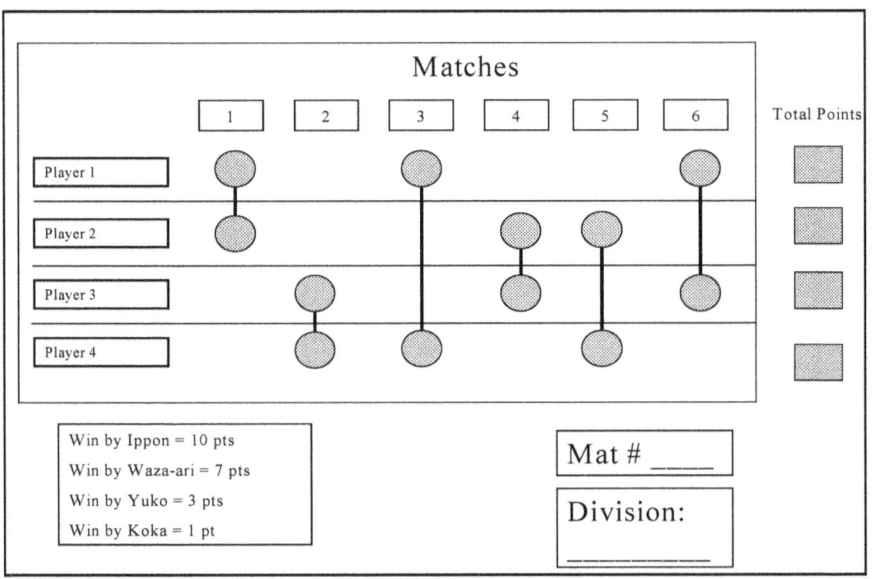

Figure 27: Four player round robin division

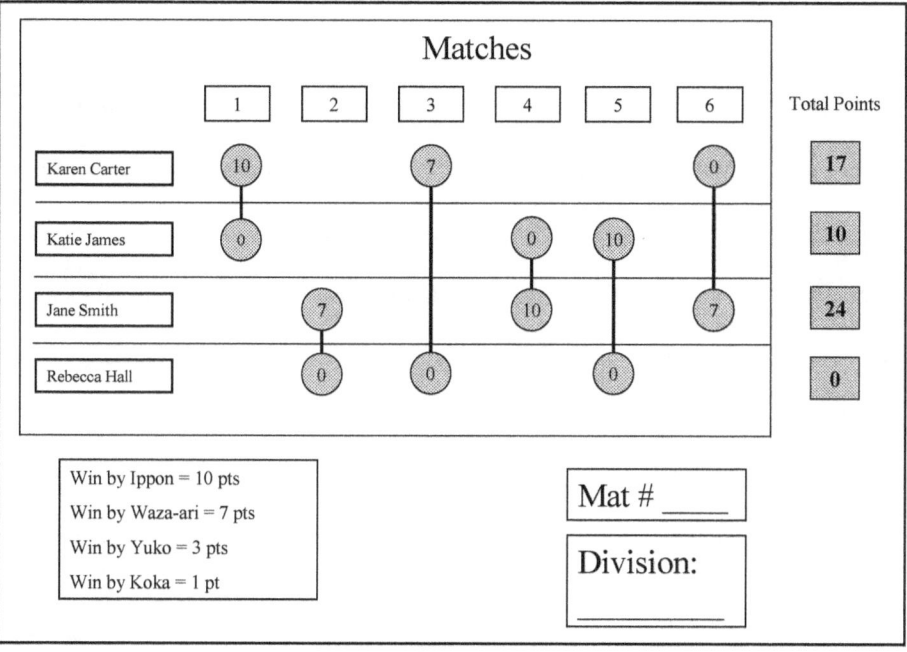

Figure 28: Example of a four person round robin division.

You can see from the examples given that the strategy of your players can be drastically altered by whether or not they are fighting in a round robin scored by points or a double elimination pool. For example, a player in a double elimination pool can afford to win with just a koka on the board in their favor. In a double elimination pool, it is only necessary to win the match to move ahead, it doesn't normally matter if the win is by ippon or by koka. In a round robin pool that is being scored on points, however, a player cannot afford to win with a koka, he or she must fight aggressively to achieve a higher score if it is the *total number of points* accumulated that wins the division, *not the number of wins*.

Hopefully, this gives you some useful information about two of the more common types of tournament divisions. For extra reading material we encourage you to obtain a copy of Byl (1990), which deals with organizing a variety of different types of tournaments and includes blank double elimination pool sheets for divisions with from three to sixty-four players. We also direct your attention to the guideline documents on the British Judo Association webpage. The B.J.A. website at www.britishjudo.org.uk/competitions/guidancedocs.php has downloadable competition sheets for a variety of pool sizes as well as repercharge tournaments.

VII. Conclusion

In this course we have examined four aspects of coaching, namely the conditions of learning, the psychology of learning, safety in the dojo and your legal responsibilities. We have also examined some of the physical principles that govern the sport/art of Judo. We do not expect you to be an expert in these areas, but we have attempted to provide information that will be of use to you in your own dojos. We also hope that you will be encouraged to continue your development as a coach and help to make Judo truly great in America. All that now remains is for you to fill in the exam and submit your paperwork in order to receive your course completion certificate.

You may contact the United States Judo Association at:

21 N. Union Boulevard
Colorado Springs, CO 80909

Or telephone us at 719-633-7750; or find the USJA Coaching Education Program on line at www.usja-judo.org.

References

Amateur Rowing Association. 2004. Good Practice in Rowing. Participant welfare, good practice and child protection policy and procedures. 26p. Available at: www.ararowing.org/youth/childprotect.php

Ames, R. 1993. Sun-Tzu: The Art of Warfare. Ballantine, New York, 321p.

American Red Cross. 1993. Standard First Aid. Staywell, Boston, 231p.

Anderson, R. A. and Anderson, J.E. 2000. Stretching. Shelter Publications, Bolinas, California, 223p.

Block, R.W. and Reece, R.M., 2005. Maltreatment. In: Crosby, A. G., and others, editors. About Children: An authoritative resource on the state of childhood today. American Association of Pediatrics, 271p.

Boy Scouts of America. 1998. The Boy Scout Handbook, 11th Edition, B.S.A. Publications, Irving, Texas, 472p.

British Judo Association. 2003. Child Protection Policy, Procedures and Guidelines. 39p. Available at www.britishjudo.org.uk/childprotection/policy.php

Bushido Zazen International Society. 2003. Child Protection Policy. Available at www.bushidozazen.dzaba.com

Byl, J. 1990. Organizing Successful Tournaments. Human Kinetics, Champaign, Illinois, 167p.

Byl, J. 2004. 101 Fun warm-up and cool-down games. Human Kinetics, Champaign, Illinois, 187p

Campbell, B. 1974. Championship Judo Drill Training. Zenbei Publishing, Sacramento, California, 128p.

Corcoran, J and Graden, J, eds. 1998. ACMA Instructor Certification Manual, Graden Media Group, St. Petersburg, Florida, 261p.

English Karate Association, 2004. Child protection Policy. Version 5, 15p. Available at www.EKGB.org.uk

Estwanik, J. 1996. Sports Medicine for Combat Arts. Boxergenics, Charlotte, North Carolina, 272p.

Flegel, M.J. 1992. Sport First Aid. Human Kinetics, Champaign, Illinois, 185p.

Football Association, 2001. Child Protection Procedures and Protection Handbook. London, England, 35p.

Gagne, R.M, Briggs, L.J., Wager, W.W. 1992. Principles of Instructional Design. Harcourt, Brace and Jovanovich, New York, 365p.

Gleeson, G. 1983. Judo Inside Out. Lepus Books, Wakefield, U.K., 155p.

Graden, J., and Callos, T. 2001 Portrait of a History in the Making: Black Belt Turns Forty. Martial Arts Professional Magazine, August, pp. 28-39.

Handal, K.A. 1992. The American Red Cross. First Aid and Safety Handbook. Little, Brown and Co., Boston, 321p.

Herbert, R. D, and Gabriel, M, 2002. Effects of stretching before and after exercising on muscle soreness and risk of injury: systematic review. British Medical Journal. Vol. 325, p.468.

Herrigel, E. 1953. Zen in the Art of Archery. Pantheon Books, New York, 90p.

Judo Canada. 1984. Coaching Certification Program, Level II. Ottawa, Canada, 168p.

Kano, J. 1986. Kodokan Judo. Kodansha International, New York, 264p.

Klein, S. B., 2002. Learning: Principles and Applications. Mc Graw Hill, New York, 564p.

Leggett, T. 1978. Zen and the Ways. Charles E. Tuttle, Vermont, 258p.

Luttgens, K, and Wells, K. F. 1989. Kinesiology: Scientific Basis of Human Motion. W.C. Brown, Dubuque, Iowa, 656p.

Martens, R. 1990. Successful Coaching. Human Kinetics, Champaign, Illinois, 237p

Mitchell, D. 1988. The Martial Arts Coaching Manual. A. and C. Black, London, 192p

Morgan, F.E. 1992. Living the Martial Way. Barricade Books, Fort Lee, New Jersey, 312p.

Nakamura, K.T. 1992. One Day, One Lifetime. World Seido Karate Organization, New York, 196p.

National Coaching Certification Program. 1979. Coaching Theory: Level 2. Canada.

Nauta, B. 1996. Illustrated Judo Techniques. United States Judo Association, Colorado Springs, Colorado, 93p.

Ormond, J. E., 1999. Human Learning. Third edition, Prentice Hall, New Jersey, 557p.

Powers, S. K, and Howley, E. T. 1990. Exercise Physiology: Theory and application to fitness and performance. W. C. Brown., Dubuque, Iowa, 539p

Robbins, A. 1986. Unlimited Power. Simon and Schuster, New York, 425p.

Watanabe, J., and Avakian, L. 1960. The Secrets of Judo. Charles E. Tuttle, Vermont, 186p

Weers, G. 1995. USJA Level I & III Coach Certification Course. United States Judo Association. Colorado Springs, 60 p.;89p.

Weers, G. 2003. The Fundamental Skills of Judo, Weers Publishing, Illinois, 122p.

Wilen, W., et al. 2000. Dynamics of Effective Teaching. Longman, New York, 397p.

YMCA – Ireland, 2002. 3.2 Child Protection Policy: Northern Ireland, 36p. Available at www.ymca-ireland.org

Appendices

Appendix 1: Information about the United States Judo Association Coaching Education Program

About the Coaching Courses and the Levels Offered

The USJA coach is a person who has decided to work on the front lines in developing Judo in America. Each level of coach should network with other coaches and seek mentors from amongst the higher-level coaches. Mentoring ensures that all coaches receive guidance that will aid in the process of moving through the coaching program levels. It will be the responsibility of certified coaching program instructors, however, to administer the actual course delivery process.

LEVEL I:

In an ideal situation, the Level I coach would be an assistant instructor within a club, however, many club coaches may find themselves running a dojo after having completed the Level I course. As such the Level I coach should be concerned with how the process of learning occurs and how the nature of the learning environment aids the process of learning. The Level I coach should have a mentor, who would normally be the main club coach or a head instructor. The candidate for Level I certification must hold a minimum rank of SANKYU. The Level I course content includes:

- Conditions of Learning
- Psychology of Learning
- Safety in the Dojo

- General
- Warm-up
- Stretching
- Cool-down
- Legal Considerations
  - Discrimination
  - Harassment
  - Negligence
- Physical Principles
- Tournaments

LEVEL II

The Level II coach should be capable of performing the functions of a club coach. The Level II coach needs to understand issues related to curriculum development, lesson planning and syllabus building as well as how to improve the fitness levels of his or her students. The Level II coach would need to increase his or her understanding of communication skills, be able to act as a mentor for Level I coaches and hold a minimum rank of SHODAN. The level II course contains the following elements:

- Conditions of Fitness
  - Energy Systems
  - Endurance
  - Flexibility
  - Strength

- Curriculum Building
  - Lesson Planning
  - Testing Cycles
  - Age-appropriate Teaching
- Communication Skills
  - Quality Communication
  - Reinforcement
  - Reward
  - Motivation
  - Challenges, Progress and Retention
  - Working with Children
  - Working with Parents

LEVEL III

The Level III coach is a highly experienced club coach, the chief instructor of a club or a regionally recognized coach who is successful at long-term development of his or her players. As such, the Level III coach will need to understand all issues of long term retention including aspects of nutrition and fitness, training cycles, ancillary training and injury management. The Level III coach would act as a mentor for Level II coaches and be able to give positive advice that would help to improve the student retention levels of a Level II coach. Although harder than the previous levels of the program, most coaches should be able to earn a Level III certificate if they are willing to create long-range training plans for their players and themselves. Candidates for Level III must hold a minimum rank of SHODAN. The course content for a Level III candidate will include the following topics.

- Building a Team
- Long-range Development/Personal Development
- Training Principles
- Training Cycles
- Goal Setting,
- Training Plans
- Record Keeping
- Personal Integrated Attack System (PIAS)
- Ancillary Training
- Nutrition
- Injury

LEVEL IV

The Level IV is a nationally recognized coach who may also be a specialist in his or her area of expertise. The Level IV coach would be the person to whom other coaches would turn when they want to develop programs for specific populations within the Judo community. As such the Level IV coach is a resource for the development of lower level coaches. Only coaches, who hold a minimum rank of NIDAN and who have achieved pre-eminence in their field, should earn this level of certificate. All candidates for this level of certification must be mentored by a certified Level IV Course Instructor who has been successful in the arena in which the candidate seeks certification.

- Training/Coaching/Teaching Special populations
- The local to national competitor
- The international competitor
- The collegiate player
- The recreational player
- The kata specialist/competitor
- Age-specific teaching for junior populations 6-12 and 12-16
- Age-specific teaching for older adults 40+
- Gender-specific teaching for adults
- Specific teaching for self-defense and personal security
- Examination by project work, thesis presentations and record keeping for chosen group. In lieu of a thesis, the Level IV candidate may elect to give a presentation at the USJA Symposium in which he or she can outline the steps that led to the creation of a successful program in their own field of expertise.

Requirements for Level I

Any member of the USJA, USJI or USJF may take Level I coaching course who meets the following criteria:

    i.   Minimum rank of Sankyu,
    ii.   Minimum of twelve months of Judo training,

Any member of another martial arts organization who wishes to take the USJA Coaching Education Courses is welcome to do so.

What Will It Take To Get This Course Done?

The Level I course is designed to be completed in less than eight hours. Many of you who take the course at a USJA clinic or camp will probably complete the course in less than five hours. Obviously, there is a lot more information in this manual than you can assimilate in such a short period of time. In the words of Douglas Adams **"Don't Panic."** The manual is designed as a resource to which you can and should return after the course is finished.

We recognize that for many of you taking the Level I course, this is the first exposure that you have had to learning how to teach. That's fine. What we want you to come away with is an *idea* of the various aspects of coaching. It is for this reason that the test at the end is designed as a take-home, open book examination. We want you to pass.

How Do I Pass The Level I Course?

In order to become certified as a Level I coach, you must either

- Attend a Level I coaching clinic and pass the associated exam at the seventy percentile (70%) mark or better at the clinic site.

- Or, attend a Level I coaching clinic and pass the associated exam at the seventy-five percentile (75%) mark or better at your own convenience after the conclusion of the clinic.

- Or, complete the course through distance learning by passing the associated test at the eighty percentile (80%) mark.

- The test for the Level 1 course is available from the chair of the USJA Coaching Education Committee.

What Do I Do To Get A Course Completion Certificate?

Applications for course completion certificates must include:

- The candidate test

- The application form

- The testing and certificate fee

- Proof of current USJA/USJI/USJF membership

- A current resume of all Judo and other relevant activities

When Do I Need To Renew My Certificate?

The Level I course completion certificate is issued for a period of three years. At the end of that time you will be notified that your course completion certificate is about to expire. You may elect to either renew your Level I credential through distance learning or by attending a USJA Level I coaching course at a USJA sanctioned clinic, camp or symposium, or, if you meet the requirements, move up to Level II by passing the Level II course at a clinic or by home study. If you elect none of these options, your coaching credential will expire and your name will be removed for the coach list on the USJA website. We strongly urge you to maintain a current certificate of course completion, to protect you from issues of liability.

About the Course Instructor Levels Offered

The **Course Instructors** are those coaches who have met the requirements for the appropriate level and subsequently been approved by the Coaching Education Committee to teach the program courses. **Course Instructors** are capable of teaching the required course materials and signing off on course completion forms for coaching candidates. If you like, these are the "trainers of the trainers." These are the **only** people who have the authority to offer program clinics and recommend that certificates of course completion be issued.

To become a Course Instructor, a candidate must be at least twenty-one years old. He or she must also be a current, active member of the USJA in good standing and have been actively teaching as the coach of a club for not less than five years. Proof of age, organizational affiliation and coaching activity will be required before certification will be issued. Course Instructor candidates must also meet the requirements outlined for each level or may petition for special consideration using one of the other options listed at the end of this section.

The certification of Course Instructors will be reviewed every three years with loss of certification if no activity shown in three-year period (to be read as having not certified any new coaches). Appeal subject to review by Coach Education Committee

LEVEL I COURSE INSTRUCTOR

- Minimum rank Shodan
- Must have successfully completed the Coach Level II course
- Must hold a passing grade of not less than 85% for the Level I exam
- Must submit coaching/martial arts resume
- Must have current First Aid/CPR course (will accept: ASEP, AHA, Red Cross, University course in general safety methods or similar with transcript and syllabus, other with proof of content).

LEVEL II COURSE INSTRUCTOR

- Minimum rank Nidan
- Must have successfully completed the Coach Level III course
- Must hold a passing grade of not less than 90% for the Level II exam
- Must submit coaching/martial arts resume
- Must have current First Aid/CPR course.

LEVEL III COURSE INSTRUCTOR

- Minimum rank Sandan
- Must have successfully completed the Coach Level III course
- Must hold a passing grade of not less than 95% for the Level III exam
- Must submit coaching/martial arts resume
- Must have current First Aid/CPR course

LEVEL IV COURSE INSTRUCTOR

- Minimum rank Sandan
- Must have successfully completed the Coach Level IV course
- Must hold a passing grade of not less than 95% for the Level III exam
- Must submit coaching/martial arts resume
- Must have current First Aid/CPR course

OTHER OPTIONS

People with appropriate credentials can petition to become a Course Instructor based upon a willingness to pass all written exams for the USJA courses that the candidate wishes to teach and submission of credentials to be reviewed by the Coach Education Committee. Therefore:

- Must be willing to pass all USJA coaching exams up to level being sought as instructor **AND ALSO**

- Petition Coach Education Committee with evidence of a baccalaureate degree or higher in Health, PE, or related field, must be willing to submit transcript of degree from an accredited institution of higher education. **OR**

- Petition Coach Education Committee with evidence of ACMA (American Council on Martial Arts) coach certification with submission of certificate **OR**

- Petition Coach Education Committee with evidence of ASEP (American Sports Education Program) Instructor courses (Both leader level courses or higher) with submission of certification **OR**

- Petition Coach Education Committee with evidence of other teaching credential in sports/recreation/physical activity from an appropriate, recognized coach certification organization (national or international) with certificate and/or syllabus of content, e.g. NCCP (National Coach Certification Program of Canada).

Appendix 2: Sample Warning, Waiver, Release of Liability, Assumption of Risk and Agreement to Participate

THIS AGREEMENT MUST BE SIGNED BY ALL MEMBERS WHO WISH TO PARTICIPATE IN ANY _____ SANCTIONED EVENT.

In consideration of being allowed to participate in any way in the sanctioned events of the _____, I, _____:

1. Recognize and understand that martial arts training is a physical contact activity and that my participation might result in serious injury, including permanent disability or death, and severe social and economic loss.
2. Recognize and understand that such risk may be due to not only my own actions, but also the action, inaction or negligence of others, the regulations of participation, or the conditions of the premises, or of any of the equipment used.
3. Recognize that there may be other risks that are not known to me or to others or not reasonably foreseeable at this time.
4. Agree to inspect the facilities, equipment and pairings prior to participation. I will immediately inform an instructor if I believe that anything is unsafe or beyond my capability and refuse to participate.
5. Assume all the foregoing risks and accept personal responsibility for any damages that may result from injury, permanent disability or death.
6. Enter martial arts training and/or competition entirely of my own free will and understand the importance of following the rules of training and competition. I have been given a copy of the rules and regulations of the _____ and agree to abide by the instructions given therein.
7. I certify that I am in good physical condition, and have no disease, injury or other condition that would either impair my performance or physical and mental well-being during intense training practice and/or competition, or pose a risk to others.
8. Grant permission in case of injury to have a doctor, nurse, athletic training or other emergency medical personnel provide me with medical assistance or treatment for such injury.
9. Release, waive, discharge and covenant not to sue, the United States Judo Association, its affiliated organizations and national governing bodies, their officers, instructors and personnel, other members of the organizations, participants, supervisors, coaches, sponsoring organizations or their agents, and if applicable, owners and leasers of the premises from any and all liability to the undersigned, his or her heirs and next of kin for any and all claims, demands, losses and damages which may be sustained and suffered on account

of injury, including death or damage to property, caused or alleged to be caused in whole or in part by the negligence of the releasees or otherwise.

I HAVE READ THE ABOVE WARNING, WAIVER, RELEASE AND AGREEMENT TO PARTICIPATE. I UNDERSTAND ITS CONTENTS AND DO HEREBY SIGN IT VOLUNTARILY.

Printed Name	Signature	Date
Printed Name of Parent or Guardian if under ____	Signature	Date
Printed Name of Parent or Guardian if under ____	Signature	Date

Appendix 3: Sample Risk Agreement

AUTHORITY TO TREAT

I, the undersigned, give the instructors, staff and responsible adults the power to authorize medical or other treatment of the student named _____, subject to the limitations listed below, if any. If I am not the named student, I am the parent, guardian or responsible adult for the named student, and I have legal right to grant this power. Treatment may be made without regard to whether I or any other parent, guardian or responsible adult has been contacted or has consented to the specific treatment, provided it does not conflict with the limitations outlined below. This authority begins on the date signed and continues indefinitely.
Limitations to treatment: _____

Information of Medical Significance: _____

By granting my authorization, I assume responsibilities for all decisions made, provided they are reasonable decisions under the circumstances based on the knowledge and understanding of the person making the decisions, and I trust their judgment and offer the benefit of the doubt to them in any claim or legal proceeding. This presumption may only be overcome by clear and convincing evidence that they acted with malice or willful gross negligence, and if so they may still be liable
Signature and Date:_____

Print Name and Relationship (if other than self): _____

I understand that the instructors, senior students, or others may have some skills in first aid, CPR, and, at their discretion, I authorize them to use those skills and techniques to assist in any circumstance in which they judge their skills would be necessary or helpful.

Initials: _____

ADVISORY OF RIGHTS AND RESPONSIBILITIES

Safety is not the sole responsibility of instructors and staff. Everyone in class is responsible for their own safety and the safety of those around them.

All students have the right and responsibility to excuse themselves from any exercise they believe will be harmful to them. All students must evaluate each situation in the context of their skill and current physical condition, and conduct each drill in a manner that is safe. If an instructor gives an instruction that is unsafe for the student, it is the student's responsibility to inform the instructor that the activity may be unsafe. The instructor will routinely excuse the student from unsafe exercises and drills. The instructor may ask or an explanation, and the student is expected to provide one.

All students have the responsibility to train and conduct themselves in a manner that helps all students and instructors remain safe. Students must give those who are training enough room to avoid interfering and avoid being accidentally struck by someone else practicing, which is especially important when others are practicing with weapons.

In the event of an injury, students have the right and responsibility to evaluate the extent of harm, stopping what they are doing even if it includes a partner, and determining if it is safe to continue. Unless a student is certain that further practice will not create or worsen a problem, all students are encouraged to stop what they are doing and inform the instructor. In the event of a serious injury or the appearance of a serious injury, all students, instructors, staff and visitors, notably parents, have the right to call a stop to a particular training exercise.

If a student notes an unsafe training situation, which may include a student performing a skill incorrectly, a student not showing due regard for the safety of others, a defective piece of training equipment, a potentially dangerous obstacle or condition on the floor, or anything else that may cause or lead to harm of students, instructors, visitors or guests, then the student is expected to correct the situation if it is within his ability or to notify an instructor or staff member immediately. If something is simple to correct, such as removing an obstacle from the floor, the student should correct the situation. If the situation may require the authority of the instructor or staff, or if it is not a simple matter, then an instructor or staff member should be notified immediately.

Initials: _____

ASSUMPTION OF RESPONSIBILITIES AND RISK

Martial arts training is a potentially dangerous activity. Bumps, bruises, scrapes, scratches and soreness are commonplace, and most students will encounter this sort of minor injury from time to time in their training. More serious injuries are possible, including sprains, strains, twists, cramps, and injuries of similar magnitude, and the student can be expected to encounter these injuries infrequently. The possibility of more serious injury exists, including fractured bones, broken bones, torn ligaments, though not all students encounter such serious injuries. There remains, despite safety precautions, the remote possibility of crippling or death, though this is certainly not expected in this martial arts class.

I understand the above statement of risk, and I understand the rights and responsibilities of students. I assume responsibility for my on safety (or the safety of my child), understanding and accepting the risks involved with martial arts training. Even if the instructor has informed me that no serious injuries have ever happened in this school or with any of the instructors, I understand that this does not mean that there is no possibility of harm. By assuming this risk, I completely absolve all instructors, staff, guests, students, landlords, management companies and any and all other parties of liability for my harm, unless intentionally caused in criminal conduct.

Initials: _____

NOTICE AND CONSENT TO INSTRUCTORS

This school seeks to make use of highly trained professional instructors, with both expertise and experience both in the art(s) that we teach and in teaching. Classes may be taught by the head instructor or any other qualified instructor. Should an instructor be unavailable for a given class, a junior instructor, senior student or guest instructor may teach. The choice of the instructor is left to the discretion of the school.

I understand that I may not always have the instructor I desire, but I shall seek to learn form whomever is teaching, to show the respect due the position of teacher to whomever is teaching, and to conduct myself in accordance with the etiquette established at this school. I understand that I have the responsibility for my own safety without regard to who may be teaching the class. I specifically consent to any instructor the school, instructors or staff feel are sufficiently qualifies by standards they set to teach the class. I specifically understand and agree that the full force of this document applies no matter who is teaching.

Initials: _____

NOTICE OF PHYSICAL CONTACT

Complete martial arts training involves a wide variety of skills. While practicing these skills, students may have contact with any portion of the body. The groin may be the target of kicks, strikes or grabs. The chest, buttocks, groin or any part of the body may be contacted by any part of the training partner's body during training with martial arts techniques, or incidentally contacted while performing a martial arts technique which targets another portion of the body.

When male and female students train together, or when adult and minor students train together, and in any other training combination, the purpose and intent of the school, instructors and staff is to provide an environment for all students to learn and practice martial arts and self-defense. Students are expected to conduct themselves appropriately at all times to ensure the best training results for everyone. Should any student feel that a training partner is engaging in contact beyond the scope of training, or a training partner is taking undue and unacceptable advantage of training contact, or if a student is made uncomfortable by any training exercise or partner, then that student has the right to withdraw from the exercise or drill. If the contact of a training partner appears inappropriate, the student should inform the instructor privately. If the conduct of the training partner or any training partner appears criminal, then the instructor should be informed and the authorities may be notified either by the student or the instructor, or both.

Initials: _____

CONSENT TO PHYSICAL CONTACT

I understand the nature of physical contact in martial arts training, and I understand that I have the right to immediately withdraw from any exercise or drill in which the contact of any party seems beyond the scope of training and makes me uncomfortable. I agree to abide by school etiquette in all matters pertaining to training, and I shall not in any way conduct myself inappropriately or take inappropriate advantage of the contact martial arts training allows.

Initials: _____

INDEMNIFICATION BY PARENTS
Applicable only to parents enrolling a minor child.

I agree not to bring any claim or suit against the school, instructors, staff, guests, students, landlord, or any other parties on behalf of my child for any injury or harm sustained by any event short of a criminal act, and then only the criminal shall be the subject of such a suit. I further agree that I will not cause to be brought, nor encourage a claim or suit. I also agree not to cooperate in the bringing of such a suit or claim except insofar as I may be legally required to do so. Finally, I shall indemnify the school, instructors, staff, guests, students, and any and all additional defendants covered by this agreement for all judgments, costs, attorney fees and other expenses incurred as a result of a breach of this agreement.

Initials: _____

ARBITRATION CLAUSE

Should any dispute arise between me, my child, or anyone acting on behalf of my child, regarding this school, then I specifically agree that the dispute shall be resolved in binding arbitration. Should a suit be filed in Court, I specifically authorize the Court to order the case to binding arbitration.

SEVERABILITY

If any clause, sentence, phrase or statement is found unenforceable or invalid by any Court of Law, the remainder of the document shall remain valid enforceable and the invalid clause, sentence, phrase or statement shall be considered struck from the document.

DURABILITY

This document is effective from the date signed with no expiration. Furthermore, the terms of this document are retroactive to the beginning of training and visiting this school if this document was signed after that date.

I have read this document, and I understand the content of it. I agree to abide by the terms of it.

Student Signature and Date:

_____

For minor students:

Parent Signature and Date:

_____

Parent Signature and Date:

_____

Witness Signature and Date:

_____

Appendix 4: Sample Health History Form

Name:_____ Age: _____
Birth Date: _____

Past and Present Health History (check all that apply)
_____ Diseases of the heart and arteries
_____ Abnormal electrocardiogram ECG
_____ High Blood pressure
_____ Angina pectoris (chest pain)
_____ Epilepsy
_____ Stroke
_____ Anemia
_____ Abnormal Chest X-ray
_____ Cancer
_____ Asthma or other lung disease
_____ Orthopedic or musculo-skeletal problems
_____ Diabetes

If any of the above are checked, please explain and indicate any recommendations your doctor has made regarding exercise:
_____
_____
_____
_____

Is there a family history of heart disease, hypertension, stroke, diabetes, lung disease or epilepsy?

_____ Yes _____ No

Level of Physical Activity:

Yes ____ No ____ Are you currently involved in a REGULAR aerobic exercise program?

Yes ____ No ____ Are you currently involved in a weight training program?

Yes ____ No ____ Do you regularly perform stretching exercises?

What best describes your level of physical activity during the last 4-6 weeks
_____ Very Active
_____ Moderately Active
_____ Occasionally Active
_____ Inactive

Appendix 5: Sample Blood Policy

To protect the members of this dojo against disease, we have adopted the following policy, which is intended to minimize the risk of transmission of all blood borne pathogens during activities. Current available medical evidence suggests that the risk of transmission during the type of contact that occurs in most martial arts activities is extremely slight. Organizations such as the NCAA and the U.S. Olympic Committee have concurred that the already slight risk of transmission can be reduced still further by the use of "Universal Precautions". The _____ will observe these precautions for the protection of everyone concerned:

1. If you have any open wounds or sores, you must clean them with suitable antiseptic and cover them securely with a leak proof dressing before practice. If your hands or feet have broken skin, suitable gloves or shoes may be worn to cover the affected areas. If you notice that someone has an open wound, please remind them of their obligation before training with that person.

2. If a bleeding wound, even minor, occurs during training, the student shall stop practicing immediately and leave the mat area until the bleeding has stopped or has been dressed. Latex gloves are provided in the First Aid kit if a person needs assistance with dressing a wound. Hands should be washed with soap and hot water once the gloves have been removed. All gloves and used dressings should be placed in a leak proof plastic bag and disposed of carefully. Minor bloodstains on the student's uniform should be treated with disinfectant. Major bloodstains require that the uniform be removed and a clean one worn before the student can return to training.

3. If you come into contact with the blood of another person, stop training immediately, leave the training area and wash the exposed area with soap and hot water.

4. If blood is on the mat, the training partner shall insure that no one inadvertently comes into contact with the blood. The blood should be cleaned up with the disinfectant provided for that purpose. Any person involved in this process should wear latex gloves and wash their hands with soap and hot water

as soon as the gloves are removed. Contaminated items should be disposed of as set out in paragraph 2.

5. If you suffer from a blood borne pathogen disorder, it is your personal responsibility to notify your training partners. As with any medical condition, it is important to check with your family doctor to make sure that it is reasonable for you to participate.

6. Finally, there are other diseases and illnesses, beside from those transmitted through blood. You are reminded that you are responsible not only for your health and safety, but also the health and safety of those with whom you train. If you know or suspect that you have a disease or illness, which might infect other, refrain from training until you are no longer a risk to others. This self defense and consideration of yourself and your fellow students is your responsibility and a part of your training. It is embodied within the code of behavior that we espouse and is part of the spirit of Judo we study.

Appendix 6: Sample Double Elimination Pool Sheet

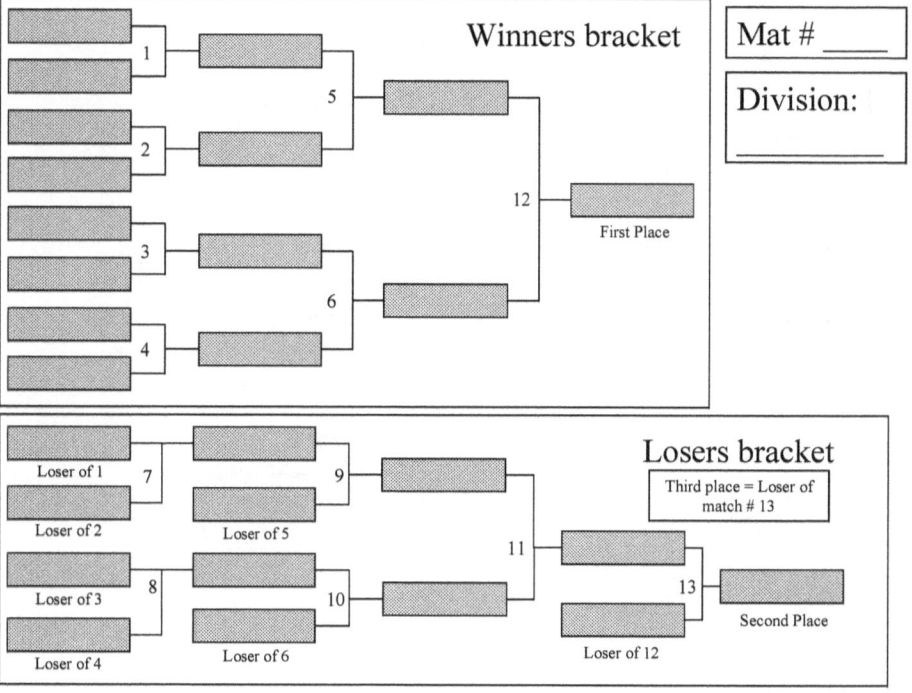

Appendix 7: Sample Four Player Round Robin Pool Sheet

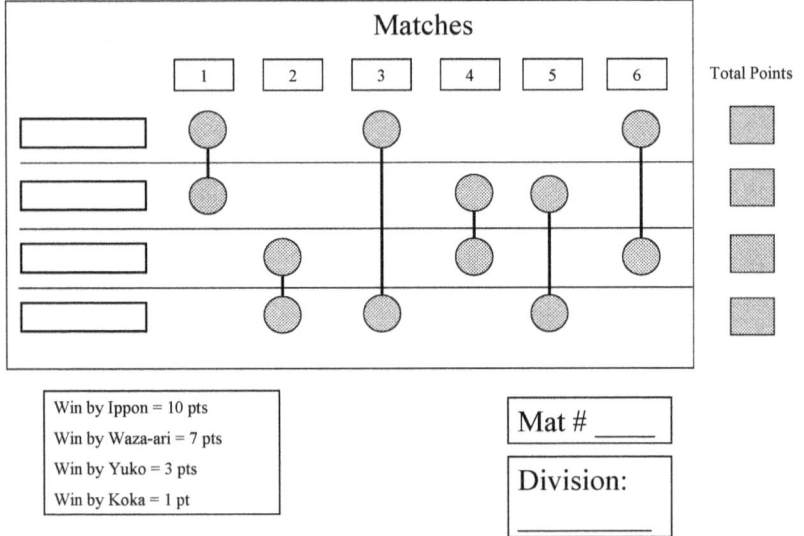

Win by Ippon = 10 pts
Win by Waza-ari = 7 pts
Win by Yuko = 3 pts
Win by Koka = 1 pt

Mat # _____

Division: _____

www.ingramcontent.com/pod-product-compliance
Lightning Source LLC
Chambersburg PA
CBHW022104160426
43198CB00008B/343